Intellectual Property and Law of Ideas

Ideas are the fuel of industry and the entertainment business. Likewise, manufacturers receive suggestions for new products or improvements to existing products, and retailers frequently receive ideas for new marketing campaigns. Many ideas are not new and may be used by anyone without the risk of incurring any legal liability, but some ideas are novel and valuable. If the originator of a potentially useful idea does not have the financial resources to exploit the idea, he or she may submit it to another, with the expectation of receiving compensation if the idea is used. Although an extensive body of intellectual property law exists to protect the rights of inventors, authors, and businesses that own valuable brands or confidential proprietary information, raw ideas receive no protection. Nevertheless, the originator of a potentially useful and marketable idea is not without legal recourse. The courts have developed, through a long line of common law precedents, legal protection for novel and concrete ideas under certain circumstances. The originator of an idea can rely on contract law, whereby the recipient may expressly or impliedly agree to pay for the idea. Alternatively, if the idea is disclosed in confidence, its unauthorized use by the recipient allows the originator of the idea to recover compensation. Finally, some courts have treated the ownership of ideas as quasi-property rights.

Kurt M. Saunders is a Professor and Chair of the Department of Business Law at California State University, Northridge. He received his B.S. in Economics from Carnegie Mellon University, a J.D. from the University of Pittsburgh, and an LL.M. in Intellectual Property Law from George Washington University. He is the author of the books, *Intellectual Property Law: Legal Aspects of Innovation and Competition* (2016) and *Practical Internet Law for Business* (Artech 2001), as well as numerous law review and journal articles on intellectual property law, business and commercial law, internet law, and legal education. He is currently the Chair of the Department of Business Law at California State University and teaches courses in intellectual property law, business law, estates and trusts law, and international business law. Prior to his academic career, he was an attorney in Pennsylvania, with his main areas of practice in business planning, intellectual property, and wills and estates law.

Routledge Research in Intellectual Property
Available:

Biodiversity, Genetic Resources and Intellectual Property
Developments in Access and Benefit Sharing
Edited by Kamalesh Adhikari and Charles Lawson

Pharmaceutical Patent Protection and World Trade Law
The Unresolved Problem of Access to Medicines
Jae Sundaram

Patent Pools, Competition Law and Biotechnology
Devdatta Malshe

Copyright Law and Derivative Works
Regulating Creativity
Omri Rachum-Twaig

The Patentability of Software
Software as Mathematics
Anton Hughes

Annotated Leading Trademark Cases in Major Asian Jurisdictions
Edited by Kung-Chung Liu

SEPs, SSOs and FRAND
Asian and Global Perspectives on Fostering Innovation in Interconnectivity
Edited by Kung-Chung Liu and Reto M. Hilty

Towards an Ecological Intellectual Property
Reconfiguring Relationships Between People and Plants in Ecuador
David Jefferson

The Transformation of EU Geographical Indications Law
The Present, Past and Future of the Origin Link
Andrea Zappalaglio

For more information about this series, please visit https://www.routledge.com/Routledge-Research-in-Intellectual-Property/book-series/INTELLPROP

Intellectual Property and the Law of Ideas

Kurt M. Saunders

LONDON AND NEW YORK

First published 2021
by Routledge
2 Park Square, Milton Park, Abingdon, Oxon OX14 4RN

and by Routledge
52 Vanderbilt Avenue, New York, NY 10017

Routledge is an imprint of the Taylor & Francis Group, an informa business

British Library Cataloguing-in-Publication Data
A catalogue record for this book is available from the British Library

Library of Congress Cataloging-in-Publication Data
A catalog record has been requested for this book

ISBN: 978-0-367-07507-1 (hbk)
ISBN: 978-0-429-02108-4 (ebk)

Typeset in Times
by SPi Global, India

To My Brother, Craig

"Everything is what it is, and not another thing."
– Joseph, Bishop Butler, SERMONS (1726)

Contents

List of Tables *viii*
Preface *ix*

1 Introduction to the law of ideas **1**

2 Legal theories of idea protection **5**
Contract law 5
Breach of express contract 6
Breach of implied contract 7
Unjust enrichment and quasi-contract 10
Breach of confidence or confidential relationship 11
Misappropriation of property 12

3 Intellectual property protection and preemption **17**
Patent law 17
Copyright law 19
Trademark law 20
Trade secret law 22
Federal preemption of state law theories of idea protection 25
Patent preemption 26
Copyright preemption 28
Trade secret preemption 31

4 Requirements for idea protection **37**
The novelty requirement 37
The concreteness requirement 41

5 Scope of liability for idea theft **47**
Recipient's use of the idea 47
The "Blurt-Out" defense 50
The independent development defense 51

6 Comparative approaches to idea protection **54**
Protection of ideas under international intellectual property law 54
Protection of ideas under national laws 56

7 Practical aspects of idea submissions **61**
Idea providers: The nondisclosure agreement 61
Idea recipients: The idea submission agreement 63

Selected bibliography on the law of ideas *69*

Index *71*

Tables

2.1 Legal Theories of Idea Protection 14
3.1 Types of Intellectual Property and Protection for Ideas 25
4.1 Requirements for Idea Protection 44

Preface

Ideas are at the center of all of our inventive, creative, and commercial activities. Defining the contours of the law of ideas, however, has often proved to be an elusive endeavor. It is a body of law that exists just outside of the domain of traditional intellectual property law, yet it lies within its orbit. It is composed of disparate legal theories drawn from the law of contracts, property, and moral rights. In addition, it is embodied in an accumulation of judicial precedents, some of which are contradictory and imprecise, and some of which are tied to a particular jurisdiction.

Nevertheless, given the importance of ideas to our economy and to our culture, and given that no cumulative source on this topic had been published, it occurred to me that the time was right for a book on the law of ideas. It would be a book that would provide guidance to idea originators and idea recipients, and serve as a source of explanation and analysis for legal researchers and practitioners. In other words, this was the idea that inspired me to write a book on the law of ideas. I am hopeful that I have succeeded in achieving these aims. More importantly, I hope the contents of this book are of use to you in the development and diffusion of your own ideas.

Kurt M. Saunders

1 Introduction to the law of ideas

Valuable ideas take many directions – ideas for new or improved products, marketing strategies, advertising slogans, manufacturing processes, television show formats and movie plots, to name a few. A valuable idea can be the source of a new revenue stream or it can be the entrepreneurial spark for a new business venture. The idea might emerge from a sudden flash of genius, or it might be the product of considered research and reflection. The source of an idea may be internal, like those from employees, or external, such as those from an interested customer or an inspired inventor or creator.

What is an idea? Is an idea a "thing," or merely the design or premonition of a thing? The dictionary tells us that an "idea" means a formulated thought, a conception. Indeed, the word "idea" is derived from the Greek term "idein," which means a form or pattern.[1] Ideas, as it has been famously said, are as free as the air.[2] The proposition that ideas cannot be owned, and that they dwell only in the public domain, was most prominently advocated by Thomas Jefferson, who wrote:

> If nature has made any one thing less susceptible than all others of exclusive property, it is the action of the thinking power called an idea, which an individual may exclusively possess as long as he keeps it to himself; but the moment it is divulged, it forces itself into the possession of every one, and the receiver cannot dispossess himself of it. Its peculiar character, too, is that no one possesses the less, because every other possesses the whole of it. He who receives an idea from me, receives instruction himself without lessening mine; as he who lights his taper at mine, receives light without darkening me. That ideas should freely spread from one to another over the globe, for the moral and mutual instruction of man, and improvement of his condition, seems to have been peculiarly and benevolently designed by nature, when she made them,

> like fire, expansible over all space, without lessening their density in any point, and like the air in which we breathe, move, and have our physical being, incapable of confinement or exclusive appropriation.[3]

Jefferson's statement is often used to argue that ideas are nonrivalrous because they are intangible. Unlike a pair of shoes or a car, which are rivalrous because they can only be worn or driven by one person at a time, ideas are nonrivalrous because one person's use of an idea does not prevent others from using it as well at the same time. Perhaps ideas, like information, want to be free?[4] If ideas are truly the building blocks of invention and creative expression, perhaps it is best to consign ideas to the public domain so as not to increase the cost to others and inhibit further inventive and creative activity? On the other hand, those who generate potentially valuable ideas quite rightly will ask: if there is no reward for ideas, why bother creating or disclosing them? In other words, as John Perry Barlow once asked, "[h]ow are we going to get paid for the work we do with our minds?"[5]

A related problem is assessing the value of an idea. Transactions in ideas – and much of the law of ideas itself – are concerned with addressing "Arrow's Information Paradox," as named for Nobel Prize economist Kenneth Arrow. He posited that a potential purchaser of valuable information wants to know it in sufficient detail so as to be able to determine its value before deciding whether to purchase it or not. However, once the potential purchaser has acquired this detailed information, the provider of the information has effectively given it away for free.[6] The paradox is that the purchaser cannot assess the value of the information until it has been disclosed, but after it has been disclosed, there is no reason to pay for it. Providers of information, as a result, will have no incentive to disclose it.

Arrow's Paradox applies to ideas in that interested parties cannot efficiently purchase or sell an idea without valuing it. However, the prospective purchaser cannot value an idea without the seller first disclosing it. The paradox can be resolved by means of intellectual property protection, which offers legal protection to certain types of information before they are disclosed. In fact, the paradox serves as one of the core rationales for patent protection.[7] The problem with ideas themselves is that an idea, without something more, does not qualify for intellectual property protection. Without something more, an idea is neither patentable nor copyrightable.

Assuming that the idea is valuable but does not qualify for protection as intellectual property, how then to protect it from being stolen if it is revealed? The story of how Mark Zuckerberg allegedly misappropriated the idea for Facebook from his college roommates provides a cautionary tale.[8] One solution is to bring it to market as fast as possible, or at least faster than one's competitors might. However, what if the idea originator lacks the capital or resources to develop the idea? Many highly creative and inventive individuals lack the ability or financial resources to convert their ideas into functional and practical form.

The next best solution may be to sell the idea to one who can make use of it. What can go wrong with that? The court dockets are replete with cases telling stories with unhappy endings:

> An expert in children's development and emotional intelligence conceived of an idea for a television series featuring five characters that are color-coded anthropomorphic emotions called the "Moodsters," accompanied by a line of toys and books about the characters. After sharing the idea with Disney with no response, Disney began development of its movie *Inside Out*, which centered on five anthropomorphized emotions that live inside the mind of an 11-year-old girl named Riley.[9]
>
> An entrepreneur believed that he had an ingenious idea for a new social media sensation – an app that would allow professional basketball fans to make predictions about National Basketball Association games and to win prizes for correct predictions. He pitched the idea to the NBA's head of emerging technology, but was politely told that the NBA was not interested. Years later, he discovered that the NBA had released a new app called "Pick 3" allowing fans to predict players, points, and a winning score.[10]
>
> Pursuant to a mutual nondisclosure agreement with a manufacturer, a consumer product designer developed a concept and prototype of a portable clothes dryer and provided it to the manufacturer. After negotiations with the manufacturer failed to lead to an agreement to purchase and commercialize the device, the manufacturer began producing and advertising a similar portable garment drying device on Twitter and the Home Shopping Network.[11]

Whether the issue is about protecting an idea, disclosing and selling it, or finding a remedy because the recipient has stolen it, an idea originator or submitter is likely to turn to the law. In such cases, the law of ideas may offer a means of protection when intellectual property law does not. The law of ideas is the area of law involving employees, customers, inventors, and authors, who submit ideas capable of being reduced to practical application to businesses.[12] It is a somewhat amorphous amalgam of contract law, property law, and tort law precedents that has been stitched together by courts over the years. The law has come to treat certain ideas as not quite intellectual property, but cousins to it. The chapters that follow explore the range and particularities of this area of law, focusing on both the requirements for protection and the remedies for misappropriation, while also considering the practical aspects involved in submitting or receiving ideas.

Notes

1 Webster's New Twentieth Century Dictionary 901 (2nd ed. 1981).
2 Desny v. Wilder, 46 Cal.2d 715, 731 (1956).
3 5 Thomas Jefferson, *The Writings of Thomas Jefferson: Being His Autobiography* 180 (1854).
4 *See* Stewart Brand, *Whole Earth Review* 49 (May 1985).
5 John Perry Barlow, The Economy of Ideas, *Wired* (Mar. 1, 1994).
6 Kenneth J. Arrow, Economic Welfare and the Allocation of Resources for Invention, in The Rate and Direction of Inventive Activity: Economic and Social Factors 615 (Nat'l Bureau of Econ. Research ed., 1962) ("[T]here is a fundamental paradox in the determination of demand for information; its value for the purchaser is not known until he knows the information, but then he has in effect acquired it without cost.").
7 In fact, an inventor may publicly disclose an invention and retain the right to the patent if he or she files an application within one year of the disclosure. 17 U.S.C. § 102(b). Similarly, trade secret protection offers at least a partial solution to Arrow's Paradox by offering an incentive for confidential disclosure of information. *See* Mark A. Lemley, The Surprising Virtues of Treating Trade Secrets as IP Rights, 61 *Stan. L. Rev*. 311, 336 (2008).
8 *See* Nicholas Carlson, How Mark Zuckerberg Hacked into Rival ConnectU in 2004, *Business Insider* (Mar. 5, 2010).
9 *See* Davis v. Walt Disney Co., 958 F.3d 767 (9th Cir. 2020) (dismissing copyright infringement and breach of implied contract claims).
10 *See* Norris v. NBA Properties, Inc., 2020 WL 1877808 (S.D.N.Y. 2020) ().
11 *See* Town & Country Linen Corp. v. Ingenious Designs, LLC, 436 F. Supp.3d 653 (S.D.N.Y. 2020) (dismissing claims for copyright and patent infringement).
12 *See* Restatement (Third) of Unfair Competition § 39 cmt. h (1995).

2 Legal theories of idea protection

An enforceable legal obligation to pay for ideas is most often based on state common law such as contract law, or in some cases on a duty of confidentiality or on property law. This chapter examines each of these theories in detail and provide case illustrations in which courts applied the theory. Contract-based theories involve either an express contract between the idea originator and recipient, or when there is no express contract, an implied contract based on the surrounding circumstances, industry custom, and any prior course of dealing. Some courts have considered claims grounded in quasi-contract and unjust enrichment.

An alternative claim for compensation arises when there has been a breach of confidential relationship due to the defendant's use of another's idea for his or her own benefit. Similarly, where the originator disclosed the idea in confidence, acting in good faith and trusting that the recipient would act in good faith as well, then the recipient is bound not to use or disclose the idea to others. A minority of jurisdictions recognize a property-like interest in ideas akin to an intellectual property right. In such cases, if the recipient makes unauthorized use of the idea, the originator can bring an action for tortious misappropriation, a claim similar to theft.

Contract law

The law of contracts has often been used to recognize legal rights in ideas and to enforce those rights in idea theft cases. A contract is an agreement, best considered in terms of a bargain or a legally enforceable promise or set of promises between two parties.[1] The contract represents correlative rights and duties between the parties. Each party has the duty to perform as agreed and each party has the right to performance by the other. Moreover, by means of the contract, each party receives a benefit from their agreement and each party incurs a detriment due to the agreement. This also represents the required element of consideration, or bargained-for exchange of value between the parties.[2] The recipient of an idea can obtain a benefit from not having to invest time and money in developing the idea or pursuing it from other sources, or by being able to implement the idea sooner rather than later.[3]

Mutual assent between the parties is essential.[4] A contract is formed when one party makes an offer and the other accepts the offer.[5] This process is measured by an objective standard based on the reasonable understanding of the parties' actions and expressions indicating agreement.[6] When the originator of a valuable idea bases a claim on contract law, he or she must prove the existence of an agreement that creates an obligation on the part of the recipient to pay compensation for receipt and use of the idea. Mutual assent arises when the idea originator makes an offer, either expressly or impliedly, by submitting or disclosing an idea with the expectation that the recipient will pay for it. When the recipient explicitly accepts the offer, or uses the idea for his or her own benefit, then a contract arises and the recipient is obligated to pay for it. If the parties have entered into an express contract as to the disclosure and subsequent use of the idea, courts generally enforce their agreement. Even if there was no express contract, the courts will determine whether one can be implied based on the conduct of the parties and the surrounding facts and circumstances. Irrespective of whether the contract is express or implied, the obligation to pay for use of the idea must be definite and mutually understood between the provider and the recipient.

Breach of express contract

An express contract is an agreement in which the terms are stated explicitly, either orally or in writing, by the parties at the time it was made.[7] As to idea submissions, an express contract results if, before or at the time of disclosure, the provider of an idea states that disclosure of the idea is on condition that he or she will be compensated if the recipient uses the idea and the recipient understands this condition and voluntarily accepts disclosure. For instance, suppose that an idea originator promises to disclose her idea in return for the recipient's promise to pay a certain amount of compensation if he uses the idea. If the recipient accepts this offer, an enforceable express contract has arisen. The disclosure of the idea and the value obtained from the disclosure serves as consideration for the contract.

An example of an express contract involving an entertainment idea can be found in the case of *Buchwald v. Paramount Pictures Corp.*[8] The plaintiff, Buchwald, wrote a short treatment describing his concept for a movie to be entitled "King for a Day" concerning a despotic African prince who visits the United States. During the visit, the prince is deposed, deserted by his entourage, and left destitute in a ghetto, where he marries a woman who has befriended him. Buchwald entered into an express contract with Paramount Pictures transferring "the sole and exclusive motion picture and other rights" to the concept. The agreement also stated that Buchwald would be compensated if Paramount produced a movie "based upon" his story idea. Although it initially pursued development of the idea, Paramount later abandoned the project. Subsequently, Paramount released the movie "Coming to America," about a wealthy and pampered African prince who comes to America to find a wife. During his visit, his property is stolen and he begins living in a slum area where he meets and marries his true love. After the movie's release, Buchwald sued for breach of express contract on the basis that "Coming to America" was "based upon" his concept. The court agreed, holding that Paramount had breached the contract because it had access to Buchwald's treatment and the movie "Coming to America" was substantially similar to "King for a Day."

Additionally, the parties may agree that the idea provider will be paid for the disclosure alone, regardless of whether the recipient decides to use the idea. From a practical standpoint, however, this would be unusual. In most circumstances, an idea originator is unlikely to reveal his or her idea before knowing that the recipient has agreed to pay for it, and one who might be offered an idea is unlikely to promise to pay for it before it is disclosed. Finally, some express contracts must be reduced to written form in compliance with the Statute of Frauds.[9] According to the Statute of Frauds, oral contracts, which by their terms, cannot be fully performed within one year of the date on which the agreement was made, are unenforceable unless in writing.[10] Therefore, if there is an express contract requiring disclosure of the idea more than one year later, or an option to implement the idea beyond one year from the date on which the agreement was made, then the contract must be in writing. If the contract is capable of being performed within one year, it need not be in writing.

Breach of implied contract

If the parties to an idea submission have not entered into an express contract to pay for use of the idea, a court may recognize an implied contract, sometimes referred to as an implied-in-fact contract, based upon the surrounding facts and circumstances of the case. More specifically, when the facts and circumstances of their interaction indicate that the parties have reached an understanding that the recipient will pay for the idea in return for its disclosure, the court will infer that a mutual agreement exists. Although implied contracts are similar to express contracts in that each requires that the parties demonstrate objective intent to agree, in an implied contract mutual assent by the parties is communicated by their conduct rather than their written or oral promises.[11]

The landmark case involving implied contracts and the protection of ideas is *Desny v. Wilder*.[12] Desny, a screenwriter, telephoned the office of Billy Wilder, a producer at Paramount Pictures, to pitch an idea for a movie based on an actual event involving a man trapped in an underground cave. Wilder's secretary advised Desny to prepare a short synopsis of the story and, two days later, he called again and dictated the synopsis to her over the phone. Desny stated that he expected to be paid if his story idea was used and she assured him that he would be compensated. Subsequently, Paramount released a movie entitled "Ace in the Hole" based on the same idea. After the studio denied his demand for compensation, Desny sued and the court recognized his claim for breach of implied contract. According to the court, the provider of an idea may pursue a contract-based claim only if "(a) before or after disclosure [he or she] has obtained an express promise to pay, or (b) the circumstances preceding and attending disclosure, together with the conduct of the offeree acting with knowledge of the circumstances, show a promise of the type usually referred to as 'implied' or 'implied-in fact.'"

The courts have noted that when the conduct of the parties indicates that the recipient of an idea solicited it or voluntarily accepted disclosure knowing that the provider expected to be compensated for its use, an implied contract has been formed even without an explicit promise to pay for the idea.[13] For instance, a disclosure at a business meeting where the provider has been invited to submit or "pitch" the idea is a context in which the recipient is likely to have understood that the provider expects to be compensated if the idea is used.[14] On the other hand, it is unlikely that such an understanding would arise where the idea was mentioned in conversation at a holiday party or during a shared ride in a taxi, nor would a public notice or listing stating general interest in particular projects likely to imply a promise to pay for idea submissions.[15]

In *Forest Park Pictures v. Universal Television Network, Inc.*,[16] for instance, the court reasoned that an implied promise to pay for an idea for a television series can be based on industry custom when the defendant kept the series treatment the plaintiff had submitted, scheduled a meeting with plaintiff, and allowed the plaintiff to pitch the idea uninterrupted.[17] Likewise, submission of the idea within the context of negotiations to purchase it would be relevant. In *Landsberg v. Scrabble Crossword Game Players, Inc.*,[18] the plaintiff disclosed an idea for a strategy book on playing the game Scrabble to the defendant in confidence. Afterwards, they entered into negotiations for the rights to the idea. During the negotiations, the defendant requested a second copy of the plaintiff's manuscript and used it to prepare its own book. The court held that this conduct may result in an implied contract to pay for the idea.

However, the submission of an unsolicited idea alone is not sufficient to lead to an implied contract, and courts will not imply a contract merely because the idea submitted is valuable. As the court in *Desny* explained, "[u]nless the offeree has opportunity to reject he cannot be said to accept." In addition, when an unsolicited idea is disclosed before the recipient knew and agreed that compensation was a condition for use of the idea, the courts will not find an implied contract. This occurs when the idea provider simply "blurts out" the idea, as happened in *Keane v. Fox Television Stations, Inc.*[19] In that case, the plaintiff developed an idea for a televised talent show entitled "American Idol" and prepared a treatment and other information describing the idea, mass-mailed it to prospective financial investors and production companies, and posted it on the Internet to generate interest. One of the recipients later developed and sold the concept for the "American Idol" talent show to Fox Television. The court dismissed the breach of implied contract claim on the grounds that he had "blurted out" his idea while seeking sponsors and had not communicated that he expected compensation in return for disclosing his idea.[20]

In a similar case, *Faris v. Enberg*,[21] the plaintiff contacted and later met with Richard Enberg, a well-known sports announcer, to discuss an idea for a sports quiz show, explaining the format for the show and suggesting that Enberg serve as the host of the show. When a similar sports quiz show featuring Enberg as host later appeared, the plaintiff sued for breach of implied contract. The court rejected the breach of implied contract and breach of confidence claims because the plaintiff's conduct did not indicate that he was attempting to sell his idea to Enberg and because Enberg did not solicit the idea, nor did the plaintiff inform Enberg that the idea was being disclosed in confidence, and he and Enberg had no business relationship from which a duty of confidentiality could be inferred. Conversely, where the recipient receives advance notice of an unsolicited idea submission with the expectation of compensation and fails to refuse it before disclosure, the courts are more willing to imply a contract based on this conduct.[22]

Unjust enrichment and quasi-contract

Another claim that is sometimes asserted in idea theft cases is unjust enrichment, which is based on the theory of quasi-contract. Suppose that someone develops an idea for marketing a particular product and submits it unsolicited to a manufacturer, who implements it with great success without compensating the idea submitter. Although there is no contractual relationship between the parties, a court might be persuaded to imply as a matter of law an obligation by the idea recipient, who knowingly accepted the idea and benefitted from it, to pay the idea submitter the reasonable value of the idea. This is an equitable remedy invoked in order to prevent injustice. In order to prove a claim for unjust enrichment, the plaintiff must demonstrate that he or she conferred a benefit on the defendant, who received the benefit and was enriched at the plaintiff's expense, and under the circumstances it would be unjust not to compensate the plaintiff.[23]

The plaintiff in *Werlin v. Reader's Digest Association, Inc.*,[24] wrote an article describing the bas mitzvah ceremony of a 13-year-old girl afflicted with Down's syndrome and the obstacles she overcame. Werlin submitted the article unsolicited to Reader's Digest, which did not publish it. Instead, Reader's Digest used the idea behind her article and directed one of its staff writers to independently write another article about the girl based on the same facts. Werlin brought a claim for unjust enrichment against the magazine. The court found that Reader's Digest would not have come across Werlin's article had she not submitted it, and that it had appropriated her idea by using the same topic in developing its own article. Finally, the court found that it would be unjust to allow Reader's Digest to benefit from Werlin's idea without compensating her.[25]

A quasi-contract is not really a contract at all, but rather a legal obligation imposed in order to prevent a party's unjust enrichment at the expense of another. A plaintiff who alleges an unjust enrichment claim must demonstrate that the idea is concrete and generally novel. However, the courts have been quite reluctant to impose liability on the basis of quasi-contract. For one reason, there is no mutual assent in the cases in which unjust enrichment is a viable claim. In addition, the idea submitter has disclosed his or her idea unsolicited and without prior indication or agreement by the recipient to pay for the idea. Courts often deny a remedy when the plaintiff has "blurted out" his or her idea.

Breach of confidence or confidential relationship

A claim that is related to breach of implied contract is that for breach of confidence. The provider of an idea can pursue a claim for breach of confidence when he or she has disclosed the idea to a recipient in confidence, and the recipient later discloses it to another without permission. A breach of confidence claim is based on an implied understanding between the parties that the idea was disclosed upon a condition of confidentiality and that the provider did not intend for the idea to be disclosed or used unless he or she is compensated for it in return. If the recipient agrees to accept disclosure of an idea in confidence, then he or she has an obligation not to disclose it to third parties or use it without compensating the provider.[26] The key to such claims is that the recipient must know that the idea is being disclosed in confidence before it is disclosed. There is no duty of confidentiality if the provider reveals the idea without giving notice to the recipient that the disclosure is confidential.

For instance, in *Aliotti v. R. Dakin & Co.*,[27] the plaintiff had developed a set of ideas for stuffed toy designs, which she presented to the defendant with whom she had hoped to obtain employment. The parties, however, had never discussed any obligation of confidentiality before or during the presentation. The court dismissed the plaintiff's action for breach of confidence filed after she discovered that the defendant was manufacturing stuffed toys based on her ideas because the mere disclosure of an idea does not in and of itself create a duty of confidentiality. By contrast, where the idea provider has made clear that his or her disclosure is in confidence, the courts will consider a breach of confidence claim. In *Davies v. Krasna*,[28] for example, the plaintiff's submission of a story idea for a theatrical play with a cover letter stating "for your confidential consideration" supported an inference that defendant impliedly agreed to the condition so that his disclosure and use of the idea was a breach of confidence.

Alternatively, an obligation to pay for an idea can arise because of the confidential nature of the relationship between the idea provider and the recipient. The disclosure of an idea within the context of a confidential relationship creates an inference that the idea was disclosed in confidence. Confidential relationships include agency relationships such as those between an employer and an employee, partnerships, and joint ventures between businesses.[29] A duty of confidentiality is implicit in such a relationship. For instance, an employee who learns of a valuable idea within the scope of her employment is under a duty of confidentiality not to disclose it to others. In the context of idea submissions, a confidential relationship does not result from the mere submission of an idea to another, and a confidential relationship is not a relationship in which the parties deal with one another from an equal bargaining position. Instead, there must be evidence that the idea was communicated in confidence to the recipient, or actions and conduct by and between the parties from which it can be inferred that they were in a confidential relationship. Thus, in *Thompson v. California Brewing Co.*,[30] the court held that a confidential relation existed when the plaintiff disclosed an advertising idea to promote the sale of beer to the defendant with the expectation that the defendant would compensate him for its use.

Nevertheless, the existence of a confidential relationship is not essential to a claim for breach of confidence. An idea may also be disclosed confidentially in the course of arm's-length negotiations between businesses when there is an understanding between the parties that the disclosure is confidential. For instance, in *Stewart v. World Wrestling Federation Entertainment, Inc.*,[31] the defendant's use of the plaintiff's lingerie design ideas after repeated in-person contacts and cooperative efforts between them supported a breach of confidence claim. Such an obligation of confidentiality may arise through the conduct of the parties or due to the context of the disclosure, or as a result of a notice of confidentiality appearing on documents describing the idea.[32] In *Victor G. Reiling Associates v. Fisher-Price, Inc.*,[33] a confidential relationship was formed as to the submission of an idea for a toy because the defendant had solicited ideas from outside inventors and had a practice of either returning or paying royalties for use of submitted ideas. Moreover, a duty of confidentiality can be created explicitly by an express agreement between the parties.

Misappropriation of property

The essence of property is the right to exclude others from using or possessing what one owns. Another approach to the protection of ideas that has been taken by a minority of jurisdictions is to treat them as a form of property in which the idea originator has an ownership interest. As the owner of the idea, the idea originator has the exclusive right to use or disclose the idea, or authorize others to do so. In this, there is a clear distinction between New York and California as to recognizing this type of idea protection. While the courts in both New York and California grant legal protection to ideas under express and implied contract law, New York law recognizes property rights in ideas, but California law does not.[34] Thus, plaintiffs in California courts must assert their idea theft claims as a breach of express or implied contract.

The focus of property-based theory is on the nature of the idea itself as property, rather than on the transactional relationship between the idea submitter and the recipient, which is the concern in contract-based theories. The rationale of a property-based theory of protection is that if an idea is a form property, then it can be owned and its owner has the right to exclude others from using or disclosing it without authorization. A claim for misappropriation of an idea based on property theory is analogous to the common law intentional tort of conversion, which involves the intentional exercise of dominion or control over another's personal property without his or her consent.[35] Misappropriation of an idea is the taking of property, causing its owner to suffer competitive or financial harm as a result.

Idea misappropriation cases most often turn on whether the proposed idea is sufficiently novel and concrete, both of which are fact-based inquiries.[36] In *John W. Shaw Advertising, Inc. v. Ford Motor Co.*,[37] the plaintiff had proposed an advertising plan incorporating the slogan, "Get the Feel of the Wheel" for Ford automobiles. Ford rejected the idea, but several years later adopted the slogan "Take the Wheel, Try the Feel" for the Ford passenger automobile, which the plaintiff alleged was substantially similar to the slogan it had proposed. The court refused to grant summary judgment in favor of Ford, explaining that in claims grounded upon a property interest in an idea, the idea must meet the rigorous requirements of novelty and concreteness, both of which are findings of fact that must be made at trial.

Essential to any idea misappropriation claim is proof of economic injury. In *Blackmon v. Iverson*,[38] the plaintiff proposed that Allen Iverson use "The Answer" as a nickname and for marketing purposes if he became a professional basketball player. Iverson later became a famous player in the National Basketball Association and entered into a merchandising agreement with Reebok, which sold athletic shoes and apparel featuring "The Answer" as a slogan and logo. The plaintiff was never paid any compensation from these sales and filed a misappropriation claim against Iverson. The court dismissed the claim, however, because the plaintiff failed to prove that he had suffered any loss of a competitive advantage or injury to his business interests.

Many of the cases in which courts have recognized property rights in ideas involve advertising slogans and television or radio formats.[39] Unlike contract claims, which are limited to recovery for economic harm, misappropriation claims sound in tort, allowing for the possibility that the successful plaintiff may recover punitive damages. Nevertheless, among the principal bases for idea theft claims, property theory is the least applied form of protection. Since the California Supreme Court's decision in *Desny v. Wilder*,[40] California no longer recognizes property rights in ideas and, as will be discussed in detail later, the standard of proof is quite demanding for property-based claims. The plaintiff must demonstrate that the idea is absolutely novel and the idea must be highly detailed and specific in order to be concrete and thereby warrant protection. These requirements are enough to preclude recovery in most cases. Moreover, as explained in the next chapter, there is a risk that most property-based claims will be preempted by the Copyright Act or Patent Act (Table 2.1).

Table 2.1 Legal Theories of Idea Protection

Theory	*Definition*
Express Contract	The idea submitter agrees, orally or in writing, to disclose the idea, and in exchange, before it is disclosed, the recipient agrees to compensation for use of the idea.
Implied Contract	The surrounding circumstances and conduct of the parties demonstrate that the idea recipient voluntarily accepted disclosure knowing that the submitter expected to be compensated for use of the idea.
Unjust Enrichment or Quasi-Contract	The court will imply as a matter of law an obligation by the idea recipient, who knowingly accepted the idea and benefitted from it, to pay the idea submitter the reasonable value of the idea in order to prevent injustice.
Breach of Confidence or Confidential Relationship	The idea submitter disclosed the idea in confidence or under circumstances where the recipient actually knew before the idea was disclosed that confidentiality was expected, and the recipient accepted disclosure and promised not to use or disclose the idea to others.
Misappropriation of Property	The idea submitter owns a property interest in the idea and can exclude others from making unauthorized use of it.

Notes

1 *See* Restatement (Second) of Contracts § 17.
2 *Id.* § 71.
3 *See* Khreativity Unlimited v. Mattel, Inc., 101 F. Supp.2d 177, 185 (S.D.N.Y. 2000).
4 (Second) of Contracts §§ 18 & 20.
5 *Id.* § 22.
6 *Id.* § 21.
7 *See* Colvig v. KSFO, 36 Cal. Rptr. 701 (Cal. Ct. App. 1964) (oral promise to pay $100 per week for use of an idea for a radio format created an express contract). Whether written or oral, the terms of the contract must be sufficiently definite to give rise to an enforceable agreement. *See* Sellers v. American Broadcasting Co., 668 F.2d 1207 (11th Cir. 1982) (written contract based on an idea for a story that Elvis Presley died of a drug overdose and personal physician may have been grossly negligent in over-prescribing drugs was too indefinite and vague to enforce).
8 13 U.S.P.Q.2d 1497 (Cal. Super. Ct. 1990).
9 A contract subject to the Statute of Frauds is enforceable if evidenced by any writing, signed by the party to be charged, which reasonably identifies the subject matter of the contract and which indicates that an agreement has been formed and states with its essential terms with reasonable certainty. Restatement (Second) of Contracts § 131. The issue does not usually arise in the context of implied contracts.
10 *See, e.g.*, CAL. CIV. CODE § 1624(1); *N. Y. Gen. Oblig. Law* § 5–701(a)(1).
11 *See* Restatement (Second) of Contracts § 19. However, if there is an express contract between the parties, an implied contract will not supplant it. *See* Baer v. Chase, 392 F.3d 609 (3d Cir. 2005).
12 299 P.2d 257 (Cal. 1956).
13 *See* Cole v. Phillips H. Lord, Inc., 28 N.Y.S.2d 404 (N.Y. 1941).
14 *See* Gunther-Wahl Prod., Inc. v. Mattel, Inc., 128 Cal. Rptr.2d 50 (2003) (holding that were designer of toys invited to give presentation there need not have been explicit conditioning of disclosure for pay for there to be an implied contract claim for company's later creation of highly similar toys).
15 *See* Grosso v. Miramax Film Corp., 2006 WL 6047731 (Cal. Sup. Ct. 2007) (finding that a listing in a writer's guidebook is not evidence that the defendant intended to solicit movie ideas from the general public and forward it to the studio with a promise to pay for any ideas used).
16 683 F.3d 424 (2d Cir. 2012).
17 *See also* Gunther-Wahl Prods., Inc. v. Mattel, Inc., 128 Cal. Rptr.2d 50 (Cal. Ct. App. 2002) (the recipient's request for a submission and presentation of an idea for an animated television series and related toy line led to an implied contract to pay for use of the idea); Vantage Point, Inc. v. Parker Bros., 529 F. Supp. 1204 (E.D.N.Y. 1981 (implied contracts may be based on industry custom or usage regarding use of idea submissions).
18 736 F.2d 485 (9th Cir. 1984).
19 297 F. Supp.2d 921 (S.D. Tex. 2004).
20 *See also* Klekas v. EMI Films, Inc., 198 Cal. Rptr. 296 (Cal. Ct. App. 1984) (no implied contract had been created based on solely an unsolicited submission of an idea for a movie about a soldier who returns to his

hometown after 20 years of military service to the publisher of the novelized version of the movie "The Deer Hunter").

21 158 Cal. Rptr. 704 (Cal. Ct. App. 1979).

22 *See* Donahue v. Ziv Television Prog., Inc., 54 Cal. Rptr. 130 (Cal. Ct. App. 1966).

23 *See* Reeves v. Alyeska Pipeline Serv. Co., 926 P.2d 1130, 1143 (Alaska 1996) (allowing a quasi-contract claim based on defendant's use of an idea for a visitor center).

24 528 F. Supp. 451 (S.D.N.Y. 1981).

25 *See also* Seymore v. Reader's Digest Ass'n, Inc., 493 F. Supp. 257 (S.D.N.Y. 1980); Trenton Indus. v. A. E. Peterson Mfg Co., 165 F. Supp. 523 (S. D. Cal. 1958).

26 *See* Entertainment Research Group, Inc. v. Genesis Creative Group, Inc., 122 F.3d 1211, 1227 (9th Cir. 1997) (applying California law); Fischer v. Viacom Int'l, Inc., 115 F. Supp.2d 535, 543 (D. Md. 2000) (applying New York law).

27 831 F.2d 898 (9th Cir. 1987).

28 54 Cal. Rptr. 37 (Cal. Ct. App. 1966).

29 *E.g.*, Sloan v. Mud Prods., Inc., 114 F. Supp. 451 (N.D. Okla. 1953) (joint venture).

30 310 P.2d 436 (Cal. 1957).

31 74 U.S.P.Q.2d 1024 (S.D.N.Y. 2004).

32 Industry practice can give rise to a duty of confidentiality. *See* Restatement (Third) of Unfair Competition § 41 cmt. b (1993) ("In some cases the customs of the particular business or industry may be sufficient to indicate to the recipient whether a particular disclosure is in confidence.").

33 450 F. Supp.2d 175 (D. Conn. 2006).

34 *See* Desny v. Wilder, 299 P.2d 257, 270 (Cal. 1956).

35 Restatement (Second) of Torts § 222A.

36 As the court in *Ligget & Meyer v. Meyer*, 194 N.E. 206 (Ind. Ct. App. 1935), instructed: "While we recognize that an abstract idea as such may not be the subject of a property right, yet when it takes upon itself the concrete form which we find in the instant case it is our opinion that it then becomes a property right subject to sale. Of course it must be something novel and new, in other words, one cannot claim any right in the multiplication table."

37 112 F. Supp. 121 (N.D. Ill. 1953).

38 324 F. Supp.2d 602 (E.D. Pa. 2003).

39 *See, e.g.*, Marcus Advertising, Inc. v. M. M. Fisher Assoc., Inc., 444 F.2d 1061 (7th Cir. 1971); Davies v. Carnation Co., 352 F.2d 393 (9th Cir. 1965); Boop v. Ford Motor Co., 278 F.2d 197 (7th Cir. 1960); Hamilton Nat'l Bank v. Belt, 210 F.2d 706 (D.C. Cir. 1953); Kovacs v. Mutual Broadcasting Sys., 221 P.2d 108 (Cal. 1950); Educational Sales Programs, Inc. v. Dreyfus Corp., 317 N.Y.S.2d 840 (N.Y. 1970); Cole v. Phillips H. Lord, Inc., 28 N.Y.S.2d 404 (N.Y. 1941); How J. Ryan & Assoc. v. Century Brewing Ass'n, 55 P.2d 1053 (Wash. 1936); Alevizos v. John D. & Catherine T. MacArthur Found., 764 So.2d 8 (Fla. Ct. App. 1999); Thomas v. R.J. Reynolds Tobacco Co., 38 A.2d 61 (Pa. 1944).

40 299 P.2d 257, 264–65 (Cal. 1956). *See also* Minniear v. Tors, 72 Cal. Rptr. 287 (Cal. Ct. App. 1968) (rejecting a claim for conversion on the grounds that ideas are not property rights).

3 Intellectual property protection and preemption

Traditional bodies of intellectual property law do not protect undeveloped ideas. This is true under U.S. intellectual property law as well as the laws of other countries that are members of the World Trade Organization (WTO) and therefore subject to the Trade-Related Aspects of Intellectual Property Agreement (TRIPS Agreement), a comprehensive multilateral agreement on intellectual property.[1] Neither copyright law nor patent law protects abstract ideas, regardless of how original or novel they may be. Trademark law protects branding ideas only to the extent they are commercially used and known to consumers as indicators of source. Alternatively, an idea might be maintained as a trade secret, but it must be economically valuable and be unknown to and not easily discoverable by competitors.

Where an idea has been expressly delineated or applied to solve a specific problem, claims based on state law idea protection theories will be preempted or superseded by copyright or patent law. Preemption of state law by federal law arises under the Supremacy clause of the U.S. Constitution or because of preemption provisions in federal statutes. To the extent that a claim for idea theft is equivalent to any of the exclusive rights of copyright or comes within the subject matter of patent law, it will be preempted by those federal laws. In such cases, the plaintiff must rely on copyright or patent law as the basis for his or her claim if the requirements for copyright or patent protection are met. Finally, if an idea qualifies for trade secret protection, certain tort claims are preempted.

Patent law

Patents protect applied technological inventions. The U.S. Constitution makes clear that the purpose of patent law is to promote the progress of the useful arts through disclosure of inventions in exchange for a limited term of protection.[2] According to the Patent Act, which defines the requirements for patentability, inventions that may be patented include: "any ... process, machine, manufacture, or composition of matter, or ... improvement" on any of these.[3] This definition is also in accord with article 27(1) of the TRIPS Agreement.[4] In addition, the invention must be useful, novel, and nonobvious. An invention is useful when it serves a "specific benefit,"[5] and is novel if it has never before been publicly disclosed anywhere in the world.[6] Finally, an invention is nonobvious when those knowledgeable in the field and familiar with the existing technology could not have easily conceived of it.[7] During the term of protection, a patent grants an inventor the right to exclude others from making, using, selling, or importing the invention the patent protects.[8]

Excluded from patent protection are abstract ideas, along with laws of nature, natural phenomena, and mathematical formulas. The United States Supreme Court has said these are "basic tools of scientific and technological work" that are "part of the storehouse of knowledge" that have always existed and are freely available to all.[9] The prohibition on patenting abstract ideas dates back to the nineteenth century, with the Court explaining that the originator of an idea cannot patent it without first developing a novel and nonobvious product or process that implements it.[10] More recently, the concern with patentability of abstract ideas has arisen in the context of computer software, as in *Gottschalk v. Benson*,[11] where using an algorithm for converting binary-coded decimals into binary numerals was rejected as being merely an abstract idea.[12] Similar concerns with determining whether business methods are patentable or unprotectable abstract ideas have occupied courts. The courts have declared the following business methods to be patent-ineligible abstract ideas: a method for managing a bingo game,[13] a method for crowd-funding a project in exchange for incentives,[14] and a method of pricing a product for sale.[15]

The current approach to resolving this question can be found in the Supreme Court's decision in *Alice Corp. PTY Ltd. v. CLS Bank International*,[16] which involved claims for a method for mitigating settlement risk in financial transactions using a computer as a third-party intermediary. The Court applied a two-part test: (1) is the claim directed to an abstract idea, natural phenomena, or law of nature? (2) if so, does the claim contain an inventive concept or limitation that applies the idea, natural phenomena, or law of nature? Merely using a general-purpose computer to implement the claim did not transform the idea into a patentable invention. As such, the Court ruled that the claims were directed to the abstract idea of "intermediated settlement" and therefore not eligible for patent protection. Although patent eligibility is based on what the claim recites, not simply on the idea upon which it is based, the present focus is on whether the claim is sufficiently applied or whether it is so broad so as to preclude other uses of the idea. In other words, an abstract idea is not patent-eligible because it is a general concept that is not applied to some particular apparatus or practical result.

Copyright law

A copyright, pursuant to the U.S. Copyright Act, is a set of exclusive rights granted to authors as to the ownership and use of their original works. Copyright protection extends only to the expression found in works of authorship. The types of works that may be copyrighted are: (1) literary works; (2) musical works; (3) dramatic works; (4) pantomimes and choreographic works; (5) pictorial, graphic, and sculptural works; (6) motion pictures and other creative works having both a visual and audio component; (7) sound recordings; and (8) architectural designs.[17] Copyright protection also extends to computer software, as well as compilations of data and information.[18] For example, an idea for movie can be expressed in a dramatic work such as a screenplay or in the motion picture itself.

The work must be original and fixed in a tangible medium, meaning that it was recorded or preserved in some stable, physical form.[19] For instance, a theatrical play can be fixed when written on paper, a sculpture is fixed when it is chiseled from stone, and a sound recording is fixed when stored on a flash drive. Originality is a relatively easy requirement to meet. The origin of the work must be the author, who did not copy it from another, and the work must demonstrate some minimal degree of creativity contributed by the author.[20] Copyright protection vests the moment the work is created and fixed, regardless of whether the work is published or registered.[21] Once vested, however, an author may register his or her copyright with the U.S. Copyright Office, but registration is not required for copyright protection to exist. Copyright owners have the exclusive rights to reproduce, distribute, adapt, and publicly perform and display those works.[22]

An important qualification to copyright protection is that it extends only to the *expression* found in works of authorship. It does not apply to ideas, concepts, and facts, which are in the public domain.[23] This principle, which is known as the "idea/expression dichotomy," applies to all works of authorship and is derived from the Supreme Court decision in the case of *Baker v. Selden*.[24] Selden was the author of a book explaining a new system of bookkeeping. The books described the system and included blank forms for its use. Subsequently, Baker published his own book describing the same bookkeeping system. In the suit for infringement that followed, the Supreme Court ruled that Baker had only copied Selden's idea in the form of the bookkeeping system, but not his expressive description of it. Thus, the copyright on the book did not prevent others from explaining or using the same system.

The rationale for the distinction between ideas and copyrightable expression is to encourage creativity; if ideas are the building blocks of creativity, then allowing others to freely borrow the underlying ideas and concepts used by one author allows others to create their own original expression of the idea. Furthermore, copyright protection of ideas would implicate freedom of speech since it would allow authors to suppress discussion of ideas contained in their works leading to a monopoly of those ideas. As a result, the exclusion of ideas from the scope of copyright protection is incorporated in the Copyright Act.[25] Article 9.2 of the TRIPS Agreement confirms that copyright protection extends only to expressions and not to ideas and concepts.[26]

Trademark law

A trademark is a source indicator because it identifies the origin or source of the goods or services. According to the federal Lanham Act, a trademark can be words, phrases, symbols, designs, or a combination of words, phrases, symbols or designs.[27] This scope of subject matter is consistent with state law as well as Article 15 of the TRIPS Agreement, which defines a trademark as a sign or combination of signs capable of distinguishing the goods or services of one business from another, including words, names, figures, colors, or combinations of these.[28] Trade dress, in the form of a product's color, design, or packaging, can be protected under U.S. trademark law as well.[29] In the United States, a business can obtain trademark protection under state common law or by registration under the federal trademark statute known as the Lanham Act. In order to register a trademark, a business must file an application with the U.S. Trademark Office, which will review the application and determine whether it meets the requirements for protection. One of the key requirements for protection is that the mark must be distinctive. Distinctiveness means that the mark is capable of identifying and distinguishing the goods or services of one business from those of another.[30] This occurs when the mark becomes associated in the minds of consumers with a single source for the particular goods or services in question.

Assume that an entrepreneur conceives of an idea for a trademark to use with her new product line. The products will be available and offered for sale to the public within five or six months. Does trademark law afford any protection for this idea? The answer is no; an idea or concept for a trademark is not itself a trademark. In the United States, trademark rights are gained from use of the mark, and not registration. Use means that the mark is affixed to the product or its packaging, displayed in connection with the service, or in advertising, when the goods or services are available for purchase.[31] The mere selection or adoption of a mark, even if accompanied by preparations to begin using it such as through advertising, are insufficient for claiming ownership of and applying to register the mark.[32] Instead, the mark must be used in trade and commerce such that the goods or services are publicly offered to those for whom they are intended. Without such use, consumers cannot associate the mark to the source of the goods or services, which in turn is necessary for the mark to become distinctive. Since the mark in this example is not yet in use, there is no trademark and no protection for her idea.[33]

Because the right to a mark is derived from its bona fide use, there is no property right in a trademark itself.[34] Moreover, the claimant to a trademark must establish priority of use by being the first to make bona fide use of the mark in trade and commerce.[35] While trademark law does not provide any legal protection for unused trademarks, the originator of an idea for a trademark may find some protection for trademark ideas in alternative state law theories. In *Duffy v. Charles Schwab & Co., Inc.*,[36] the plaintiff submitted a business proposal, along with an idea for the trademark "Mutual Fund Report Card," to Charles Schwab & Co. The proposal and accompanying materials were marked "Proprietary and Confidential." Although Charles Schwab reviewed and rejected the proposal, it later registered and began using the trademark. The plaintiff sued for trademark infringement and breach of confidence. The court rejected the trademark claim on the basis that the plaintiff had obtained no rights in the mark through prior use. However, the court allowed the breach of confidence claim to go to trial because the plaintiff had disclosed his proposal and idea for the trademark in confidence.

Likewise, if one conceives of an idea for a mark for a particular service, and offers to disclose it to the provider of that service in return for compensation if it is used, either expressly or under circumstances that support that expectation, then the idea submitter may have a claim for breach of express or implied contract if he or she is not paid. Finally, it is no longer possible to rely on the Lanham Act to argue that the uncredited copying of another's idea results in liability for unfair competition by making a "false designation of origin ... of goods." Such a claim is based on passing off the works of another as one's own or without proper attribution. In *Dastar Corp. v. Twentieth Century Fox Film Corp.*,[37] the Supreme Court ruled that the term "origin" in the statute referred to the source of the physical goods themselves rather than the author of the idea or expression embodied in those goods. The *Dastar* decision therefore precludes a moral right of attribution for ideas and for copyrighted works, including works in the public domain.[38]

Trade secret law

The United States has a parallel system of state and federal trade secret law. On the state level, all states but one have adopted the Uniform Trade Secrets Act (UTSA), while the Defend Trade Secrets Act is its federal equivalent. Under both laws, a trade secret is business information that has economic value and is subject to reasonable measures to maintain its secrecy.[39] This is consistent with article 39.2 of the TRIPS Agreement, which states that protection applies to undisclosed information that is secret, which has commercial value because it is secret, and which has been subject to reasonable steps to keep it secret.[40] Almost any kind of information used in a business can be a trade secret, including technical and financial data, recipes, chemical formulas, patterns, compilations of data, computer programs, devices, designs and product specifications, methods and systems, techniques, marketing plans, processes, research results, and lists of actual or potential customers or suppliers.[41]

The information must be sufficiently secret so that the firm derives actual or potential economic value as a result.[42] The value of the information must result from it being unknown and not easily discoverable.[43] To ensure that the information is not generally known or readily ascertained, the owner must take specific and affirmative steps to protect it. The owner need only take reasonable efforts to maintain the secrecy of the information.[44] Absolute secrecy is not required, and what is reasonable in each case depends on the particular circumstances, including the nature of the product or service, the state of the art in the trade or industry, and the level of risk of disclosure.[45] Trade secret protection can last indefinitely if the information remains unknown to competitors. However, unlike patent protection, once a trade secret is disclosed, even if improperly, the trade secret is lost. This is the main reason that trade secret law is considered to provide a weaker form of protection for inventions than patent law.[46]

Although the definition of trade secret is broad enough to encompass ideas as a form of information, and an idea could certainly have economic value before it is disclosed, trade secret protection is a somewhat awkward fit for idea protection. Ideas that are only novel to the recipient rather than generally novel cannot be trade secrets because they are known even though they can be protected by express contract theory. In *McKay Consulting, Inc. v. Rockingham Memorial Hospital*,[47] for instance, an idea for increasing hospital disbursement rates was readily ascertainable from published laws and regulations.[48] Likewise, ideas are developed with intent that they will be sold to someone who will put them to use. Ultimately, the idea must be disclosed to a recipient, or in some cases the idea may have been disclosed unsolicited.[49] In either case, the idea is no longer secret without some nondisclosure or confidentiality agreement in place beforehand. In *Stromback v. New Line Cinema*,[50] the court determined that a movie idea was not a trade secret because it had economic value only if it was publicly exploited, and in *Johnson v. Benjamin Moore & Co.*,[51] the court made this point about a marketing idea, explaining: "A marketing concept does not by confidentiality create a continuing competitive advantage because once it is implemented it is exposed for the world to see and for competitors to legally imitate."[52]

In recent years, however, some courts have become amenable to treating valuable ideas as trade secrets under the UTSA. In *Learning Curve Toys, Inc. v. PlayWood Toys, Inc.*,[53] the plaintiffs developed a concept for grooved wooden railroad tracks that produced a "clickety-clack" sound when toy trains ran over the track. They disclosed the idea in confidence while demonstrating a prototype of the track to a toy manufacturer. When the manufacturer later implemented the concept without compensating the plaintiffs, they sued for trade secret misappropriation. The court of appeals agreed that their idea was a trade secret because it was not generally known and because the plaintiffs had used reasonable measures to maintain its secrecy by entering into an oral confidentiality agreement with the manufacturer's representatives before demonstrating the prototype. The court noted that until their idea was disclosed through sale of the toys, it remained a trade secret.[54]

Similarly, in *Altavion, Inc. v. Konica Minolta Systems Laboratory, Inc.*,[55] Dr. Ali Moussa, the president of Altavion, developed an idea for a digital stamping technology to enable self-authentication of documents. He entered into negotiations with Konica Minolta (KMSL) pursuant to a nondisclosure agreement. While KMSL evaluated the idea, it filed patent applications claiming a similar technology, and negotiations with Altavion proved unsuccessful. Altavion filed suit alleging that his idea, the general design concepts, and the algorithms and software he had developed, were trade secrets that KMSL had misappropriated. On appeal, the court agreed that ideas may be protected as trade secrets under the California trade secrets statute. The court explained:

> The least specific and least secret level of information is Altavion's general idea for a barcode allowing for self-authentication of documents with identification of alterations. This level of information is not a protectable trade secret because the general idea was disclosed to other companies without the benefit of an NDA. At the other extreme, the most specific and secret level of information is Altavion's algorithms and source code that execute Altavion's [digital stamping technology]. Such information is unquestionably protectable by trade secret law, but it could not form the basis for Altavion's misappropriation claim because Altavion did not share its algorithms and source codes with KMSL. The middle tier of information is comprised of the design concepts that underlie Altavion's [digital stamping technology], many of which might be evident to a software end user. There is no evidence such information was disclosed to anyone other than KMSL, pursuant to an NDA, and, thus, misappropriation of these secret design concepts (separately and in combination) provide a basis for Altavion's claim.[56]

The court's rationale is instructive. General or abstract ideas cannot be trade secrets, and this is consistent with the requirement that ideas demonstrate some level of concreteness. When an idea is reduced to a functional form like source code or designs, and it is used in business, it may be protected as a trade secret if it is maintained and disclosed under conditions of confidentiality.

In considering these decisions and the requirements for trade secret protection, it appears that an idea before disclosure might be protected as property in those jurisdictions like New York that recognize this theory. If the idea is disclosed subject to a confidentiality or nondisclosure agreement, it could be protected under contract theory or lead to liability as a breach of confidence if it is misappropriated. Thus, while trade secret law can encompass ideas as trade secrets, it is important to remember that ideas and trade secrets differ fundamentally.[57] The nature of a valuable idea is to be disclosed to others so that they can exploit it, whereas the nature of a trade secret is to remain a secret,

Table 3.1 Types of Intellectual Property and Protection for Ideas

Intellectual Property	*Scope of Protection*	*Protection for Ideas*
Patents	Novel, useful, and nonobvious inventions, including processes, machines, manufactured goods, and compositions of matter	No protection for abstract ideas, only those reduced to practice
Copyrights	Original works of authorship fixed in a tangible medium of expression, including literary, musical, dramatic, artistic, choreographic, architectural works, and sound recordings	Ideas and concepts not protected, only the expression of ideas
Trademarks	Distinctive indicators of the source of goods or services, including words, names, phrases, symbols, and trade dress	No protection for ideas for trademarks, unless the mark is distinctive and used in trade or commerce
Trade Secrets	Economically valuable business information which is not known to competitors and subject to reasonable measures to maintain its secrecy	Limited protection for ideas, unless they are disclosed or readily or independently discoverable by competitors

even if the owner has not yet put it to use.[58] In an idea submission case, the idea originator desires that the recipient use the idea and the dispute involves payment for the idea. In a trade secret misappropriation case, the trade secret owner seeks compensatory damages because the defendant used or disclosed the idea improperly (Table 3.1).

Federal preemption of state law theories of idea protection

Based on the foregoing, it is perhaps somewhat misleading to state that there is no protection for ideas under patent, copyright, trademark, or trade secret law. An idea developed and reduced to a novel, useful, and nonobvious invention is patentable. An idea expressed in original and tangible form is copyrightable. The more concrete an idea is delineated, the more likely it is not an unpatentable abstract idea and the more likely it is to be copyrightable expression. A branding idea can be a trademark if it is distinctive and has been put into actual use.

Trade secret law may protect some ideas in the form of confidential information that derives economic value from remaining secret. Ideas that do not qualify for protection under patent, copyright, trademark, or trade secret law may be protected under state law under the right circumstances.

However, another issue sometimes arises due to the interplay between state law and traditional forms of intellectual property. The problem arises from the federalist system of government in the United States in which state governments share authority with the federal government. Inevitably, disputes arise when state law and federal law apply concurrently. Indeed, courts generally presume that states possess concurrent authority to regulate unless Congress has expressly displaced state law. When Congress has not done so, but state law directly conflicts with the purposes and objectives of federal law, the Supremacy clause of the United States Constitution dictates that federal law will supersede state law.[59] This is known as preemption of state law by federal law.

The effect of preemption is that the state law is rendered inapplicable and invalid. The law of preemption has been defined by a series of Supreme Court decisions regarding conflicts that have arisen between various state law rights and the federal law of patents and copyrights. These decisions reflect a balancing between the policies underlying federal intellectual property law and their impact on state sovereignty. They also provide guidance as to those instances when federal law may be held to preempt the protection of ideas under state law.

Patent preemption

Preemption in patent law becomes an issue when state law recognizes a right that resembles a patent by excluding others from using, making, or selling a particular type of invention. In the cases of *Sears, Roebuck & Co. v. Stiffel Co.*[60] and *Compco Corp. v. Day-Brite Lighting, Inc.*,[61] the defendants sold lamps and lighting fixtures that copied the designs of those sold by plaintiffs, which were patent-eligible but did not meet the novelty and nonobviousness requirements for patent protection. The plaintiffs brought claims under state unfair competition law, but on appeal to the Supreme Court, the Court held that the state law claims were preempted by federal patent law, reasoning that subject matter not sufficiently inventive to qualify for patent protection should remain in the public domain and free to be copied.

Although the initial reaction to these decisions was that they heralded the end of state law forms of intellectual property protection, the Supreme Court subsequently held in *Kewanee Oil Co. v. Bicron Corp.*[62] that a state law claim for trade secret misappropriation was not preempted by patent law. In analyzing whether there was a conflict between patent and trade secret law, the Court noted that patent law promotes innovation and the disclosure of inventions. Although one of the main purposes of patents is to encourage the disclosure of inventions to the public in exchange for the protection afforded by a patent, the Court reasoned that trade secret law also provides incentives that encourage innovation among those who do not wish to publicly disclose their inventions. There is no conflict because owners of inventions that are not patentable will not apply for a patent anyway, and owners of inventions that are likely to be patentable will usually opt for disclosure and stronger patent protection than for weaker trade secret protection.

Two later Supreme Court decisions round out the scope of federal patent preemption. In *Aronson v. Quick Point Pencil Co.*,[63] the plaintiff invented a key holder and negotiated with Quick Point to disclose her idea and grant it a license of any future patent rights she obtained in exchange for payment of royalties, whether or not she was granted a patent. Aronson was not granted a patent, and since her invention was easy to reverse engineer, Quick Point's competitors were soon selling similar products. Quick Point sought to terminate the royalty payments on the basis that the key holder was now in the public domain and the agreement was preempted by patent law. The Court disagreed, holding that there was no preemption since the free copying of a public domain invention was not harmed by enforcing the agreement. Although the key holder design was not in the public domain before the agreement, it was disclosed in confidence as part of the agreement. Had Quick Point used the design without compensating Aronson, she would have had the right to sue for breach of contract or confidence. Instead, Quick Point received a benefit from Aronson's confidential disclosure of her invention that allowed Quick Point to be the first to market the product. The agreement was willingly entered and the key holder was not in the public domain before the disclosure. As a result, enforcement of the license agreement between the two parties did not withdraw the key holder invention from the public domain and others remained free to copy it.[64]

In the other case, *Bonito Boats, Inc. v. Thunder Craft Boats, Inc.*,[65] Florida had enacted a statute that forbids the direct molding of boat hulls for the purpose of duplicating the hulls for sale in the recreational boat market. Bonito sued Thunder Craft for violating the statute and Thunder Craft argued that the statute was preempted by patent law because it interfered with the free copying of subject matter in the public domain. The Court found that the Florida statute was preempted by federal design patent law because it granted rights against making and selling the design in the same manner as provided by patent law. The statute offered this protection for an unlimited number of years to all boat hulls, including those otherwise in the public domain because patent protection had been denied or expired, as well as for designs that had been freely revealed to the public by their creators. It conflicted with patent law by offering a substantial patent-like property right in hull designs without imposing the demanding standards necessary to obtain patent protection. According to the Court, this had the effect of reducing competition and deterring inventors from disclosing their inventions and applying for patent protection.[66]

There are several overarching principles to be synthesized from these decisions. The first is that a state law claim that resembles a broad patent-like right to exclude all others from making, using, or selling an idea is more likely to be preempted because such a right would undermine the purpose of the Patent Act. Moreover, state law cannot be used to protect or withdraw subject matter already in the public domain, even if it is eligible for patent protection, because doing so would conflict with the objective of promoting competition through disclosure and innovation. Finally, the use of state law to provide limited protection to undeveloped, abstract ideas are less likely to lead to preemption because such ideas are not patent-eligible.

Copyright preemption

Like patent preemption, copyright preemption has been considered by the Supreme Court, but unlike patent preemption, it is also specifically addressed in the Copyright Act. Before 1973, sound recordings were not protected by the Copyright Act. California enacted a statute prohibiting copying of sound recordings. In *Goldstein v. California*,[67] when Goldstein was convicted under the statute for duplicating musical recordings without permission, he argued that the statute was preempted by federal copyright law. The Supreme Court disagreed, holding that Congress had not at that time included sound recordings within the scope of copyrightable subject matter, which allowed the states to provide such protection if they chose to do so.[68]

The holding in *Goldstein* was effectively codified in section 301 of the Copyright Act, enacted in 1976.[69] Under section 301, state laws protecting subject matter not within scope of that protected by the Copyright Act are not preempted.[70] Recall that the subject matter of copyright protection includes works of authorship fixed in a tangible medium.[71] Since ideas are explicitly not protected by copyright,[72] it is clear that state rights in *unfixed* ideas, such as those disclosed entirely in oral form, are not works of authorship and therefore protection of unfixed ideas under state law is not preempted. Thus, an unfixed idea for a television series pitched orally to a producer would not be within the scope of copyright and therefore a claim for misappropriation of the idea would not be preempted.[73]

However, most courts have ruled that state protection of *fixed* ideas fall within the scope of copyright for purposes of preemption, even though the subject matter of copyright excludes ideas from copyright protection.[74] For instance, in *Metrano v. Fox Broadcasting Co., Inc.*,[75] the plaintiff alleged a claim for breach of implied contract after having orally pitched an idea for a television series at a meeting. He had also presented the defendant with a treatment, index cards which detailed 17 persons and stories that could be featured on the show, tapes of people who could be featured, and other possible source materials. The court held that his implied contract claim was preempted because "his ideas expressed in the treatment, index cards, and tapes were fixed in a tangible medium as they were embodied in a form that is stable and of endurance and from which they could be perceived and reproduced."[76]

Another reason for including fixed ideas within the scope of copyright preemption is to prevent states from protecting ideas alone from copying, thereby creating a copyright-like exclusive right to the idea itself.[77] Additionally, section 301 preempts all rights equivalent to any of the exclusive rights granted to copyright owners.[78] The rights of copyright owners are the right to reproduce the work, prepare derivative works, and distribute, perform, and display copies or phonorecords to the public.[79] If a state law affords the originator of an idea the equivalent of any of these exclusive rights, it is preempted. In determining what constitutes an equivalent right of copyright, the courts apply the extra element test, which asks whether the state law requires proof of an additional element of proof that changes the nature of the action so that it is qualitatively different from an action for copyright infringement. If the state law claim is not based on any extra element beyond unauthorized copying or infringement of other copyright rights, then it is preempted.[80]

As such, the courts apply a two-part test for resolving cases when state law is preempted. First, the work of authorship in which rights are claimed must fall within the "subject matter of copyright" as defined in the Copyright Act. Second, the state law must create legal or equitable rights that are equivalent to any of the exclusive rights within the general scope of the copyright law. In addition to section 301, courts may make an independent determination as to whether a state law right conflicts with federal copyright law under the Supremacy clause of the Constitution. In doing so, the court will analyze whether the state law interferes with the purposes of copyright law. A state law that impedes the public interest in promoting the creation of expressive works and preserving the public domain is likely to be preempted.

This approach is demonstrated in *Wrench LLC v. Taco Bell Corp.*,[81] which involved the preemption of a breach of implied contract claim seeking payment for use of an idea for an advertising campaign. The plaintiffs had proposed a commercial involving a feisty talking dog known as "Psycho Chihuahua" to Taco Bell. When the parties were unable to reach an agreement, Taco Bell retained another advertising firm that claimed that it had independently created the idea of a talking Chihuahua to launch the Psycho Chihuahua campaign. Taco Bell argued that the plaintiffs' claim was preempted because their promotional materials were copyrightable works and therefore the implied contract claim was equivalent to a copyright infringement claim. However, the court of appeals ruled that the implied contract claim was not preempted because it required an implied promise to pay for the idea as an extra element not required to prove infringement.[82]

The same reasoning would apply to claims for breach of express contract – requiring the elements of offer, acceptance, and consideration not required for copyright infringement – with the exception of a claim based on breach of a promise not infringe a copyright.[83] Likewise, claims based on breach of confidence tend not to be preempted because they involve the extra element of a promise or duty of confidentiality between the parties.[84] By contrast, claims for unjust enrichment or quasi-contract are often preempted because they do not require proof of the extra element of mutual assent and are based on assertions of unauthorized copying of the plaintiff's expression of his or her idea.[85] Finally, claims based on tort law or property, such as conversion, are the most likely to be preempted because they involve unauthorized use or theft of intangible property and are essentially equivalent to a claim for copyright infringement.[86]

In sum, the Copyright Act preempts a state law claim when two conditions are satisfied. First, the subject matter of the work which is the basis for the claim must fall within the subject matter of federal copyright law. Second, the rights asserted under state law must be equivalent to the exclusive rights granted to authors under the Copyright Act. The scope of copyright preemption is broader than the scope of copyright protection so that claims based on ideas fixed in a tangible medium can be preempted even if the expression of those ideas is not copyrightable.

Trade secret preemption

Aside from federal patent and copyright preemption, if an idea that meets the requirements for trade secret protection has been misappropriated, it is possible that some claims for idea theft will be preempted by the Uniform Trade Secrets Act.[87] Preemption is addressed in section 7 of the UTSA, which states:

> (a) Except as provided in subsection (b), this [Act] displaces conflicting tort, restitutionary, and other law of this State pertaining to providing civil liability remedies for misappropriation of a trade secret.
>
> (b) This [Act] does not affect: (1) contractual or other civil liability or relief that is remedies, whether or not based upon misappropriation of a trade secret; or (2) criminal liability for other civil remedies that are not based upon misappropriation of a trade secret; or (3) criminal remedies, whether or not based upon misappropriation of a trade secret.[88]

Section 7(a) expressly displaces tort claims and claims seeking the remedy of restitution.[89] In applying this section, the courts have held that claims for torts such as conversion[90] and intentional interference with contractual relations[91] are preempted because they are based on the factual allegations supporting misappropriation of a trade secret. Thus, assuming that a novel and concrete idea is protectable as a trade secret, a claim grounded in property theory for idea theft is likely to be preempted by an accompanying trade secret misappropriation claim based on the same set of facts. This is because such a claim is essentially one derivatively based on theft of a trade secret as intangible property. On the other hand, section 7(b) states that claims based on contract are not preempted. Such claims include those for breach of an express or implied contract, such as a claim for breach of a confidentiality or nondisclosure agreement.[92] As a result, assuming that an idea qualifies as a trade secret, a claim breach of express contract or breach of implied contract brought concurrently with a trade secret misappropriation claim will not be preempted.

The case of *HDNet, LLC v. North American Boxing Council*[93] illustrates the distinction between the preemption of tort and contract claims for idea theft. The plaintiff had proposed how the parties could develop a unique branded boxing series for broadcast on cable and satellite television and considered the information to be a protectable commercial idea. The parties never reached an agreement and the plaintiff filed suit when the defendant began using the idea, asserting claims for trade secret misappropriation, breach of contract, conversion, and idea misappropriation, among others. The court, relying on the language of section 7, found that claims for misappropriation of ideas that are protected by contract are not preempted. By contrast, the court ruled that the conversion claim merely stated another allegation for misappropriation of the plaintiff's idea.

Finally, section 7 does not address preemption of other confidential information not rising to the level of trade secrets, including ideas. As such, claims for misappropriation of ideas that do not meet the requirements for trade secret protection are not preempted.[94] The UTSA also "does not apply to duties a duty imposed by law that are not dependent upon the existence of competitively significant secret information, like an agent's duty of loyalty to his or her principal."[95] Thus, a claim for breach of fiduciary duty in using or disclosing a confidential idea is not preempted by the UTSA.

Notes

1 Agreement on Trade-Related Aspects of Intellectual Property Rights, Apr. 15, 1994, Marrakesh Agreement Establishing the World Trade Organization, Annex 1C, Legal Instruments – Results of the Uruguay Round, 33 I.L.M. 1125, 1197 (1994) (hereinafter TRIPS Agreement).
2 U.S. Const. art. I, § 8, cl. 8.
3 35 U.S.C. § 101.
4 *See* TRIPS Agreement art. 27(1).
5 *See* Brenner v. Manson, 383 U.S. 519 (1966).
6 *See* 35 U.S.C. § 102.
7 *See id.* § 103.
8 35 U.S.C. § 271(a).
9 Funk Bros. Seed Co. v. Kalo Inoculant Co., 333 U.S. 127, 130 (1948).
10 *See* Rubber-Tip Pencil Co. v. Howard, 87 U.S. (20 Wall.) 498, 507 (1874).
11 409 U.S. 63 (1972).
12 The patentability of computer software was later conclusively resolved in *Diamond v. Diehr*, 450 U.S. 175 (1981), in which the Supreme Court held that if a claimed invention containing a mathematical equation applies or implements the equation to perform a function or transform it to a different state or thing, then the invention is patent-eligible. *Diehr* involved a computer-monitored process for curing synthetic rubber, which involved the use of a well-known mathematical equation, known as the Arrhenius equation. The equation itself was not patent eligible, but the equation was incorporated into a process for curing rubber. Consequently, the Court

held that the software was patentable because it claimed application of the equation as one part of the steps of the process.

13 Planet Bingo, LLC v. VKGS, LLC, 576 Fed. Appx. 1005 (Fed. Cir. 2014).
14 Kickstarter, Inc. v. Fan Funded, LLC, 2015 WL 3947178 (S.D.N.Y. 2015).
15 OIP Technologies, Inc. v. Amazon.com, Inc., 2015 WL 3622181 (Fed. Cir. 2015).
16 573 U.S. 208 (2014).
17 17 U.S.C. § 102(a).
18 *See* Feist Publ'ns, Inc. v. Rural Tel. Serv. Co., 499 U.S. 340, 345 (1991) (compilations); Computer Assocs. Int'l, Inc. v. Altai, Inc., 982 F.2d 693, 702 (2d Cir. 1992) (software).
19 17 U.S.C. § 102(a).
20 *See* Feist, 499 U.S. at 346–347.
21 Eldred v. Ashcroft, 537 U. S. 186, 195 (2003).
22 17 U.S.C. § 106.
23 *Id.* § 102(b).
24 101 U.S. 99 (1879).
25 17 U.S.C. § 102(b).
26 *See* TRIPS Agreement art. 9(1).
27 *See* 15 U.S.C. §§ 1051(a)(3), 1127 (2012).
28 *See* TRIPS Agreement art. 15(1).
29 *See* Qualitex Co. v. Jacobson Prods. Co., 514 U.S. 159 (1995). Trade dress is a type of industrial design protected under article 25.1 of the TRIPS Agreement.
30 *See* Mishawaka Rubber & Woolen Mfg. Co. v. S.S. Kresge Co., 316 U.S. 203 (1942); Zatarain's, Inc. v. Oak Grove Smokehouse, Inc., 698 F.2d 786 (5th Cir. 1983); Abercrombie & Fitch Co. v. Hunting World, Inc., 537 F.2d 4 (2d Cir. 1976).
31 *See* 15 U.S.C. § 1127 (defining "use in commerce").
32 *See* Aycock Engineering, Inc. v. Airflite, Inc., 560 F. 3d 1350 (Fed. Cir. 2009).
33 *See, e.g.*, American Express Co. v. Goetz, 515 F.3d 156 (2d Cir. 2008) (the slogan "My Life, My Card" as part of a concept for personalized credit cards to generate interest among credit card companies was not used to identify the origin of his goods or services); Parham v. Pepsico, Inc., 927 F. Supp. 177 (E.D. N.C. 1995) (no trademark rights resulted from an idea for using the term "Crystal" as a trademark because no product or service was sold using it as a mark).
34 United Drug Co. v. Theodore Rectanus Co., 248 U.S. 90, 97 (1918).
35 *See* Grupo Gigante S.A. de C.V. v. Dallo & Co., 391 F.3d 1088 (9th Cir. 2004).
36 97 F. Supp. 2d 592 (D.N.J. 2000).
37 539 U.S. 23 (2003).
38 *See* Kurt M. Saunders, *A Crusade in the Public Domain: The* Dastar *Decision,* 30 Rutgers Comp. & Tech. L. J. 161 (2004).
39 Unif. Trade Secrets Act § 1(4) (amended 1985), 14 U.L.A. 538 (2005); 18 U.S.C. § 1839(3).
40 *See* TRIPS Agreement art. 39.2.
41 *See* Roger M. Milgram, Milgram on Trade Secrets § 1.09 (2017) (examining various types of confidential information that can be protected as

trade secrets). In addition, a trade secret can be "negative" information or know-how resulting from research blind alleys, failed designs, and methods that did not work. *See* Unif. Trade Secrets Act § 1 cmt. There is no requirement that the trade secret be novel or in continuous use, or that it exist in a tangible form to be protected. *Id.*; *see also* Jones v. Ulrich, 95 N.E.2d 113 (Ill. Ct. App. 1950).

42 Unif. Trade Secrets Act § 1(4)(i) (hereinafter UTSA).

43 *Id.* § 1(4) cmt.

44 *Id.* § 1(4)(ii).

45 *See, e.g.*, Rockwell Graphic Sys., Inc. v. DEV Indus., 925 F.2d 174, 179 (7th Cir. 1991); Data Gen. Corp. v. Grumman Sys. Support Corp., 825 F. Supp. 340, 359 (D. Mass. 1993); Mason v. Jack Daniel Distillery, 518 So. 2d 130, 133 (Ala. 1987); Aries Info. Sys., Inc. v. Pac. Mgmt. Sys. Corp., 366 N.W.2d 366, 368 (Minn. Ct. App. 1985).

46 In addition, unlike trade secret law, reverse engineering and independent invention are not defenses to patent infringement. *See* Kewanee Oil Co. v. Bicron Corp., 416 U.S. 470, 490 (1974).

47 665 F. Supp.2d 626 (W.D. Va. 2009).

48 *Accord* Sikes v. McGraw-Edison Co., 665 F.2d 731 (5th Cir. 1982) (idea for a new product not a trade secret because it can be reverse engineered).

49 *See, e.g.*, Auto Channel, Inc. v. Speedvision Network, LLC, 144 F. Supp.2d 784 (W.D. Ky. 2001).

50 384 F.3d 283 (6th Cir. 2004); Rogers v. Desa Int'l, Inc., 183 F. Supp.2d 955 (E.D. Mich. 2002).

51 788 A.2d 906 (N.J. Super. 2002).

52 *Id.* at 923. *See also* Hudson Hotels Corp. v. Choice Hotels Int'l, 995 F.2d 1173 (2d Cir. 1993); Richter v. Westab, Inc., 529 F.2d 896 (6th Cir. 1976); Bulldog N.Y. LLC v. Pepsico, Inc., 8 F. Supp.3d 152 (D. Conn. 2014); Blank v. Pollack, 916 F. Supp. 165 (N.D.N.Y. 1996); Schroeder v. Cohen, 93 N.Y.S.3d 287 (N.Y. 2019).

53 342 F.3d 714 (7th Cir. 2003).

54 *Id.* at 729.

55 171 Cal. Rptr.3d 714 (Cal. Ct. App. 2014).

56 *Id.* at 734.

57 Ahlert v. Hasbro, Inc, 325 F.Supp.2d 509 (D.N.J. 2004) (when the idea is not actually used in business it is not a trade secret); Johnson v. Benjamin Moore & Co., 788 A.2d 906, 922 (N.J. Super. Ct. 2002) ("Misappropriation of ideas is a separate area of law from both patent law and trade secret law.").

58 *See* UTSA § 1 cmt.

59 U.S. Const. art. VI, cl. 2.

60 376 U.S. 225 (1964).

61 367 U.S. 234 (1964).

62 416 U.S. 470 (1974).

63 440 U.S. 257 (1979).

64 The same conclusion applies to an action for breach of a licensing agreement. *See* Universal Gym Equipment, Inc. v. ERWA Exercise Equipment Ltd., 827 F.2d 1542 (Fed. Cir. 1987) (breach of contract action for use of a patented invention after the agreement terminated not preempted).

65 489 U.S. 141 (1989).

66 *Id.* at 168.
67 412 U.S. 546 (1973).
68 *Id.* at 570.
69 17 U.S. Code § 301.
70 *Id.* § 301(a).
71 *Id.* § 101(a).
72 *Id.* § 101(b).
73 Of course, if the idea for the television series is expressed in a copy such as a detailed treatment or video with sufficient originality to qualify as a work of authorship, it is entitled to copyright protection.
74 *See* Montz v. Pilgrim Films & Television, Inc., 649 F.3d 975 (9th Cir. 2011).
75 2000 WL 979664 (C.D. Cal. 2000).
76 *Id.* at *4. *See also* Nash v. CBS, Inc., 704 F. Supp. 823 (N.D. Ill. 1989) (claim based on ideas included in a book preempted); Paul v. Paley, 588 N.Y.S.2d 897 (App. Div. 1992) (claim for theft of ideas "fleshed out" in a manuscript was preempted by copyright law).
77 *See* Katz Dochrermann & Epstein, Inc. v. Home Box Office, 1999 WL 179603, at *2 (S.D.N.Y. 1999).
78 *Id.* § 301(a).
79 *Id.* at § 106.
80 *See, e.g.*, Ritchie v. Williams, 395 F.3d 283 (6th Cir. 2005) (claim for breach of express contract preempted because it was based on public distribution and performance of copyrighted work).
81 256 F.3d 446 (6th Cir. 2001).
82 *Id.* at 456–58. *Accord* Forest Park Pictures v. Universal Television Network, Inc., 683 F.3d 424 (2d Cir. 2016); Grosso v. Miramax, 383 F.3d 965 (9th Cir. 2004). Of course, the implied agreement must precede the disclosure of the idea. *See* Reeves v. Alyeska Pipeline Serv. Co., 926 P.2d 1130, 1140 (Alaska 1996).
83 *See* Ritchie v. Williams, 395 F.3d 283, 287–88 (6th Cir. 2005); Acorn Structures, Inc. v. Swantz, 846 F.2d 923 (4th Cir. 1988); Trenton v. Infinity Broadcasting Corp., 865 F. Supp. 1416 (C.D. Cal. 1994); Ronald Litoff, Ltd. v. American Express Co., 621 F. Supp. 981, 986 (S.D.N.Y. 1985).
84 *See, e.g.*, Stewart v. World Wrestling Federation Entertainment, Inc., 2005 WL 66890 (S.D.N.Y. 2005); Smith v. Weinstein, 578 F. Supp. 1297 (S.D.N.Y. 1984). For similar reasons, claims for trade secret misappropriation avoid preemption since they involve the extra elements of reasonable secrecy and improper means. *See* Dun & Bradstreet Software Servs., Inc. v. Grace Consulting, Inc., 307 F.3d 197 (3d Cir. 2002).
85 *See, e.g.*, Montz v. Pilgrim Films & Television, Inc., 649 F.3d 975 (9th Cir. 2011) (claim for unjust enrichment preempted by copyright law); Ultra-Precision Manufacturing, Ltd. v. Ford Motor Co., 411 F.3d 1369 (Fed. Cir. 2005) (unjust enrichment claim was in essence a claim for damages for "making" and "using" the invention and preempted by patent law); Briarpatch Ltd. v. Phoenix Pictures, Inc. 373 F.3d 296 (2d Cir. 2004) (unjust enrichment claim not qualitatively different than copyright infringement); Waner v. Ford Motor Co., 331 F.3d 851 (Fed. Cir. 2003) (claim based on unjust enrichment involving an idea for truck fender line used without permission or payment was equivalent to patent infringement). *But see* Werlin v. Reader's Digest Ass'n, Inc., 528 F. Supp. 451

(S.D.N.Y. 1981) (holding that the elements and rights involved in a quasi-contract claim differ from those in copyright law).

86 *See, e.g.*, Meridian Project Sys., Inc. v. Hardin Constr. Co., 426 F. Supp.2d 1101 (E.D. Cal. 2006) (claim for conversion preempted by copyright law); Mayer v. Josiah Wedgwood & Sons, Ltd., 601 F. Supp. 1523 (S.D.N.Y. 1985) (same).

87 A trade secret owner can bring concurrent claims for trade secret misappropriation under the federal DTSA and UTSA. The DTSA expressly indicates that "[n]othing in the amendments made by this section shall be construed ... to preempt any other provision of law" and therefore does not preempt existing state trade secret laws. 18 U.S.C. § 1838.

88 UTSA § 7.

89 For a detailed discussion of the scope of preemption under the UTSA, see Richard F. Dole, *Preemption of Other State Law by the Uniform Trade Secrets Act*, 17 SMU Sci. & Tech. L. Rev. 95 (2014).

90 *See, e.g.*, Mattel, Inc. v. MGA Entm't. Inc., 782 F. Supp.2d 911 (C.D. Cal. 2011); BlueEarth Biofuels, LLC v. Hawaiian Elec. Co., 780 F.Supp.2d 1061 (D. Haw. 2011); Diamond Power Intern., Inc. v. Davidson, 540 F. Supp.2d 1322 (N.D. Ga. 2007); Mortgage Specialists, Inc. v. Davey, 904 A.2d 652 N.H. 2006).

91 *See, e.g.*, Hauck Mfg. Co. v. Astec Indus., Inc., 375 F. Supp.2d 649 (E.D. Tenn. 2004).

92 Section 7 "does not apply to duties a duty voluntarily assumed through an express or an implied-in-fact contract. The enforceability of covenants not to disclose trade secrets and covenants not to compete that are intended to protect trade secrets, for example, are governed by other law." *Id.* cmt; *see also* Digital Envoy, Inc. v. Google, Inc., 370 F. Supp.2d 1025, 1034 (N.D. Cal. 2005); Boeing Co. v. Sierracin Corp., 738 P.2d 665 (Wash. 1987).

93 972 N.E.2d 920 (Ind. Ct. App. 2008).

94 *See, e.g.*, Javo Beverage Co. v. California Extraction Ventures, Inc., 2019 WL 6467802 (S.D. Cal. 2019); Interserve, Inc. v. Fusion Garage PTE, Ltd., 2010 WL 1445553 (N.D. Cal. 2010); American Biomedical Group, Inc. v. Techtrol, Inc., 374 P.3d 820 (Okla. 2016).

95 UTSA § 7 cmt.

4 Requirements for idea protection

Not all ideas are entitled to legal protection. Many ideas are of little use because they are too abstract, while others are already known and therefore freely available. In general, to be entitled to legal protection, an idea must be novel and concrete, which are indicators that the idea has value. The novelty and concreteness requirements also allow a court to identify that an idea created by one party has not been stolen by another.[1] Ideas are novel if they are new and original, rather than obvious and well known. An idea is concrete if it is complete and detailed enough for immediate implementation. Depending on the type of claim asserted, the requirements for novelty and concreteness reflect a sliding scale. The standards are usually relaxed when the claim is based on an express contract, more demanding in claims for breach of implied contract and breach of confidence, and quite strict in property-based claims. Furthermore, the threshold requirements of novelty and concreteness allow courts to decide whether an idea is socially and economically valuable enough to justify legal protection, thereby ensuring that recipients are not required to pay for ideas that are known or unusable, and preventing claims by idea submitters who believe incorrectly that they are entitled to compensation.

The novelty requirement

An idea is novel if it is unique, original, or significantly different from one that is already known or used in the industry. This requirement differentiates a novel idea from those originated by others and those that are in the public domain. Moreover, novelty serves as evidence of the idea's economic value. In idea theft cases, this allows a court to determine whether the idea used by the defendant was the same idea submitted by the plaintiff. The defendant is not liable if the idea was obtained from another source, otherwise publicly available, or independently developed by the defendant. In other words, such an idea did not originate with the plaintiff. Ideas that are already known to the recipient, or commonly used and well known within a particular industry, are not protectable.[2] Likewise, ideas that are simply variations of familiar themes will not be considered novel. For example, in *Vent v. Mars Snackfood U.S., LLC*,[3] the court considered an idea to promote the release of the DVD version of "The Addams Family" television series with the sale of M&M's candies for Halloween as merely a variation on a basic advertising theme and not novel. In these instances, the idea is considered obvious and therefore courts will presume that the recipient already knows of it.

This proposition is further illustrated in *Murray v. National Broadcasting Co.*,[4] a case in which the plaintiff submitted an idea to the NBC television network for a show called "Father's Day," which concerned a contemporary urban African-American family starring Bill Cosby as the father. NBC responded that it was not interested in pursuing the proposal. However, "The Cosby Show" premiered four years later, with Bill Cosby as head of an African-American family in a contemporary urban setting, and Murray filed suit. The court rejected Murray's claim for lack of novelty, explaining that where "an idea consists in essence of nothing more than a variation on a basic theme – in this case, the family situation comedy – novelty cannot be found to exist."[5] Moreover, the court noted that Bill Cosby himself had earlier suggested the same idea during an interview for a newspaper.

Similarly, an idea that is an obvious adaptation or combination of ideas already known is not considered novel. The case of *Baer v. Chase*[6] provides an illustration. In *Baer*, the plaintiff was a former New Jersey county prosecutor who provided a television producer with an idea for a television series. He gave the producer a script, information, locations, and personal stories about organized crime activities and investigations. In addition, he introduced the producer to police detectives familiar with the New Jersey mafia who discussed with him actual incidents involving the mafia. The producer subsequently developed a television series entitled "The Sopranos." The plaintiff filed suit seeking compensation based on misappropriation and breach of implied contract, contending that the show was based on his concept of a series about a New Jersey mob boss. The court decided that the idea was not novel because it was merely a combination of facts and stories existing in the public domain. In reaching this conclusion, the court distinguished between genuine novelty and the exercise of creativity in selecting and combining publicly known facts and stories, which are free and available to all.[7]

As it has evolved in idea submission cases, novelty depends on the type of legal theory relied upon by the plaintiff. In cases where the parties have entered into an express contract containing a promise by the recipient to pay for use of the idea regardless of its novelty, the courts have held that proof of novelty is not required.[8] The courts reason that the contracting parties are free to decide the terms of their agreement. An idea may be of value to that particular recipient even if it is otherwise generally known. By contrast, when protection of an idea is based on implied rather than express contract, the idea only need be new to the recipient. The same is true for claims based on breach of confidence.[9] This means that the idea is novel if the recipient had not been previously aware of it. Here, novelty to the recipient represents the value of the consideration paid for disclosure of the idea. Finally, in cases based on property theory and misappropriation, the idea must be novel in the sense that it is not generally known in the industry.[10] The general novelty standard also applies in claims for unjust enrichment based on quasi-contract theory. The reason for a more demanding general novelty standard in such cases is that no one should be able to claim a property right in an idea that is in the public domain and freely available to all. In other words, general novelty establishes the aspect of ownership of the idea necessary to claim a property right in the idea.

Since the degree of novelty required depends upon the basis of legal protection, contract law may sometimes recognize enforceable legal rights in an idea where a property-based claim would not. The decision in *Nadel v. Play-By-Play Toys & Novelties, Inc.*[11] provides an illustration. In this case, a toy inventor developed a mechanism consisting of an eccentric weight attached to a motor shaft that, when placed inside of a plush toy monkey, caused the toy when placed on a flat surface to sit upright, emit sound, and spin around. He met with an executive at a toy manufacturer and demonstrated a prototype. The executive expressed interest in adapting the concept for use in its non-moving plush "Tasmanian Devil" toy, which it was producing under a license from Warner Brothers, Inc.

Despite several requests by the inventor after the meeting, the manufacturer did not return the prototype until after it had introduced its "Tornado Taz" plush toy, which also emitted sounds, sat upright, and spun around by means of an internal eccentric mechanism. The inventor sued for breach of implied contract and misappropriation, and the manufacturer responded by arguing that the idea was not protectable since it was not a novel or original concept in the toy industry. On appeal after the district court granted summary judgment in favor of the defendant, the court began its analysis by observing that general novelty in order to support a misappropriation claim does not apply to contract claims, and that "[w]hile an idea may be unoriginal or non-novel in a general sense, it may have substantial value to a particular buyer who is unaware of it and therefore willing to enter into contract to acquire and exploit it."[12] In applying the "novelty to the recipient" standard, the court stated:

> The determination of whether an idea is original or novel depends upon several factors, including, … the idea's specificity or generality (is it a generic concept or one of specific application?), its commonality (how many people know of this idea?), its uniqueness (how different is this idea from generally known ideas?), and its commercial availability (how widespread is the idea's use in the industry?).[13]

As to the misappropriation claim, the court remanded the case for the district court to determine whether the inventor's idea demonstrated general novelty or was "a merely clever or useful adaptation of existing knowledge."[14] In also remanding the implied contract claim, the court made note of the timing of the manufacturer's release of the Tornado Taz toy in relation to the date of the inventor's disclosure to the manufacturer and genuine issues of material fact that might lead to the reasonable inference that the prototype was used as a model for development of Tornado Taz.

In reaching its conclusions, the court in *Nadel* also referred to custom in the toy industry. If it is customary for most businesses in an industry to compensate those who submit a useful idea unsolicited, then courts are more likely to find an implied contract to pay for its use. For instance, in *Whitfield v. Lear*,[15] the plaintiff told a television producer that he was sending a script for a proposed television series. The producer's assistant responded that the producer had no interest in the script and that it would be forwarded to another production company. There was no further contact between the parties, but a year later, a television series premiered that was similar to that submitted by the plaintiff and produced by the same production company. In the lawsuit that followed, the court observed that it was customary in the television industry to return unsolicited scripts unopened when a studio or producer was not interested in reviewing them. However, if a studio or producer is notified that a script is forthcoming and opens and reviews it when it arrives, then the studio or producer has by custom implicitly promised to pay for the ideas if it is used.

In comparing the standard for novelty in idea protection law to other sources of intellectual property protection, it is clear that the standard is not the same as that in patent law, which requires that an invention not be disclosed or otherwise available to the public anywhere in the world before the filing date of a patent application.[16] Nor is the standard the same as that of originality required in copyright law, which simply requires that the work possess a minimal level of creativity and the author have not copied it from elsewhere.[17] Rather, the standard of novelty for ideas appears to be closer to the requirement of economic value in trade secret law, in which the inquiry is whether the subject matter is not generally known to and not readily ascertainable by competitors.[18]

Finally, in addition to differences in proof based on the legal theory asserted, there may be variations tied to the jurisdiction in which the case is brought. The *Nadel* case was decided in New York where general novelty, although required for a property-based claim, is not a requirement for an implied contract claim. Of course, the idea must be novel to the recipient to ensure that the recipient did not already know of or independently develop the same idea. In California, it is less clear. Although the California Supreme Court indicated in 1950 that novelty to the recipient is required for claims based on implied contract or breach of confidence,[19] the California Court of Appeals in more recent cases has not required novelty.[20] It is, however, possible to read these later cases as considering disclosure of the idea rather than its novelty as sufficient consideration in express contract and implied contract cases.[21]

The concreteness requirement

In addition to novelty, most courts require that an idea be concrete to some degree in order to be protectable. An idea is concrete when it is sufficiently specific or developed to be of immediate use. By contrast, ideas that are vague, abstract, or incomplete are not eligible for protection. In addition, it is easier to identify the provider of a concrete idea and distinguish it from other ideas that may have been submitted. It is not necessary that the idea be reduced to a detailed proposal in tangible form in order to be protected. As with novelty, the specific meaning of concreteness often has been tied to the particular theory of protection. Concreteness is not required when there has been an express promise by the recipient in advance to pay for an idea. The rationale is that the recipient has agreed to pay for the idea knowing that it is not concrete. When there is no express contract, the requirement of concreteness, like the requirement of novelty, provide courts with a basis for implying a contract.

However, the underlying basis for the requirement seems to be the need to understand the exact dimensions of the idea and what it encapsulates. In this sense, the requirement is analogous to the definiteness requirement found in patent law, which requires a patent applicant to disclose claims "by particularly pointing out and distinctly claiming the subject matter which the inventor ... regards as the invention."[22] Not only does the recipient have to know what is being proposed and whether it may be of use, but a court would need to be able to identify its parameters in case of litigation.[23] The more general or abstract an idea, the more difficult it is to determine if the defendant has copied the idea or independently developed it on his or her own.

As such, one approach that courts have taken in delineating concreteness is to require that the idea be specific or definite rather than vague or abstract. For instance, the plaintiff in *O'Brien v. RKO Radio Pictures, Inc.*,[24] submitted an idea for a movie about vaudeville performers at the Palace Theater in New York City with suggestions about possible story treatments. Analyzing concreteness in the context of a claim based on property theory, the court ruled that the idea was too abstract and general to be concrete. According to the court, the idea was underdeveloped because the story as described presented only some aspects of the general profession of vaudeville.

A related approach to evaluating concreteness is to assess whether the idea is complete as to its details and developed to the point of being capable of immediate use. Concrete ideas are more likely to be useful and commercially valuable, if for no other reasons that they are ready for implementation. The analogous concept is the utility requirement in patent law, which mandates that the claimed invention have a practical use and provide an identifiable benefit. Thus, ideas that can be easily reduced to a physical form are generally usable and concrete. Examples include as an idea for an artificial candle accompanied by a description and drawings depicting the product,[25] an idea for an elevator chair safety device that had been depicted in a drawing and in a model,[26] and an idea presented during an oral presentation describing a surgical device.[27]

Likewise, in *Hamilton National Bank v. Belt*,[28] the plaintiff submitted an idea for a radio program featuring performances of high school students who had been selected through an audition process and who had been recorded live before student assemblies. In addition, the program was to involve minimal conversation and would acknowledge sponsors at the start and end of the show rather than commercial spots throughout the program. The case was decided under the property theory of idea protection. In assessing whether the idea was concrete, the court considered the nature of radio broadcasting and that the idea involved an ongoing series of broadcasts rather than a single show. The court found concreteness in the details of the overall format of the proposed program, reasoning that a full script delineating specific dialogue and instructions would not be necessary in such a format.

The relevance of industry custom and practice to the issue of whether or not an idea has been presented in a concrete form is further underscored in *Fink v. Goodson-Todman Enterprises, Ltd.*[29] In that case, the plaintiff submitted a partially developed presentation of a basic concept for a television series to be entitled "The Coward" concerning a man who, after being branded a coward during World War II, is motivated to place himself in positions of peril and engage in acts of courage. Analyzing claims based on implied contract and unjust enrichment, the court held that the idea was sufficiently concrete because it was customary to submit such presentations in the television industry.

By contrast, the idea at issue in *Smith v. Recrion*[30] was not considered to be sufficiently concrete. The plaintiff was a keno writer employed by a luxury Las Vegas hotel who decided that a recreational vehicle park constructed and operated as a part of the luxury hotel would be a profitable idea. After developing a brochure describing his idea, he arranged for and had a meeting with the hotel manager. Following his presentation, the plaintiff indicated that he desired to be compensated in the form of an unspecified amount of money or by participation in the venture in an executive capacity. The hotel expressed no interest in the proposal and the plaintiff's further attempts to discuss the idea were rebuffed.

Two years later, however, the hotel opened a recreational vehicle park known as "Camperland" adjacent to the hotel. After the opening of Camperland, asserting that the hotel had implemented his idea, the plaintiff made several demands for compensation; all of which were refused. He then sued for damages, claiming he was entitled to compensation based upon express contract and implied contract theories. The court held that his idea did not meet the test of concreteness because the brochure was not capable of immediate use without any additional embellishment. Rather, the brochure presented a raw idea of a recreational vehicle park, but was not ripe for implementation because it still required extensive investigation, research, and planning.

Most likely, had the plaintiff in *Smith* presented a set of blueprints for the project, along with a marketing plan, and a detailed budget proposal during his presentation, his idea would have met the test of concreteness. Perhaps he lacked the skills or knowledge to put together such a proposal? If so, at least one court has cited an idea submitter's lack of technical knowledge in fleshing out the details of his idea for a video gambling card game as further evidence of its lack of concreteness.[31] Similarly, in the context of ideas for advertising slogans, the court in *Bailey v. Haberle Congress Brewing Co.*,[32] held that an unsolicited submission of an advertising slogan alone was not concrete. By contrast, in *Healey v. R.H. Macy & Co.*,[33] the plaintiff submitted a slogan, along with a complete advertising plan in writing, featuring the slogan, drawings and sketches, and written advertising material. The court concluded that the idea had been reduced to a concrete form.

The form in which the idea is submitted is not determinative in evaluating its concreteness. As several of the cases previously described, an idea is concrete if it has been communicated in a tangible, perceivable form such as a written description, prototype, sketch or diagram, or a finished product. Even an idea presented informally, such as in a letter, can be sufficiently concrete.[34] Moreover, the courts have ruled that an oral presentation of an idea can be concrete if it is sufficiently understandable and developed to be usable.[35] Finally, at least one prominent jurisdiction does not require concreteness to protect an idea under the implied contract theory. In *Chandler v. Roach*,[36] the California Court of Appeals rejected the need for concreteness in evaluating whether an idea is protectable. *Chandler* involved an idea for a television series based on the activities of the public defender's office. The court rejected imposing a concreteness requirement for claims based on implied contract, seeing it as limited to idea protection based on property theory, which is no longer applicable law in California (Table 4.1).

Table 4.1 Requirements for Idea Protection

Legal Theory	*Novelty*	*Concreteness*
Express Contract	Not required	Not required
Implied Contract	Must be novel to the recipient	Required
Breach of Confidence	Must be novel to the recipient	Required
Unjust Enrichment and Quasi-Contract	Must be generally novel	Required
Property	Must be generally novel	Required

Notes

1 Sorbee Int'l Ltd. v. Chubb Custom Ins. Co., 735 A.2d. 712, 714 (Pa. Super. Ct. 1999).
2 *See, e.g.*, All Pro Sports Camp, Inc. v. Walt Disney Co., 727 So.2d 363 (Fla. Ct. App. 1999) (idea of multi-purpose sport complexes was widely known and not novel); Ring v. Estee Lauder, Inc., 702 F. Supp. 76 (S.D.N.Y. 1988) (idea to promote sales of cosmetics by video recording makeovers of customers by sales representatives not novel since video recordings were commonly used to demonstrate self-improvement techniques); Oasis Music, Inc. v. 900 USA, Inc., 614 N.Y.S.2d 878 (N.Y. Sup. Ct. 1994) (idea for an interactive game with sound effects, nonlinear plot sequence, and use of personal identification numbers for players not novel since similar games already on the market).
3 611 F. Supp.2d 333 (S.D. N.Y. 2009).
4 844 F.2d 988 (2d Cir. 1988).
5 *Id.* at 993.
6 392 F.3d 609 (3d Cir. 2004).
7 *See also* Bram v. Dannon Milk Prods. 307 N.Y.S.2d 571 (App. Div. 1970) (concept of depicting an infant in a high chair eating and enjoying yogurt lacked novelty and had been used by defendants and their competitors prior to its submission).
8 *See, e.g.*, Apfel v. Prudential-Bache Sec., Inc., 616 N.E.2d 1095 (N.Y. Ct. App. 1993); Donahue v. Ziv Television Programs, Inc., 54 Cal. Rptr. 130 (Cal. Ct. App. 1966); Krisel v. Duran, 258 F. Supp. 845 (S.D.N.Y. 1966).
9 *See, e.g.*, Sokol Holdings, Inc. v. BMB Munai, Inc., 726 F. Supp.2d 291 (S.D.N.Y. 2010); Fink v. Goodson-Todman Enters., Ltd., 66 Cal. Rptr. 679 (Cal. Ct. Ap.. 1970).
10 *E.g.*, McGhan v. Ebersol, 608 F. Supp. 277 (S.D.N.Y. 1985) (idea of a music video television program featuring interviews with and behind-the-scenes footage of performers was simply an adaptation of existing industry practices).
11 208 F.3d 368 (2d Cir. 2000).
12 *Id.* at 378.
13 *Id. See also* Duffy v. Charles Schwab & Co., 123 F. Supp.2d 802 (D.N.J. 2000).
14 *Id.*
15 751 F.2d 90 (2d Cir. 1984).
16 *See* 35 U.S.C. § 102(a).
17 *See* 17 U.S.C. § 102(a); *see also* Feist Publ'ns., Inc. v. Rural Tel. Serv. Co., Inc., 499 U.S. 340, 347 (1991).
18 *See* Unif. Trade Secrets Act § 1(4), 14 U.L.A. 433 (1985). *See also* Restatement (Third) of Unfair Competition § 39 (1995).
19 *See* Stanley v. Columbia Broadcasting Sys., Inc., 221 P.2d 73 (Cal. 1950).
20 *See, e.g.*, Blaustein v. Burton, 88 Cal. Rptr. 319 (Cal. Ct. App. 1970); Fisk v. Goodson-Todman Ent., Ltd., 88 Cal. Rptr. 679 (Cal. Ct. App. 1970); Chandler v. Roach, 319 P.2d 776 (Cal. Ct. App. 1957).
21 For further discussion of the issue, see William O. Knox, *The Role of Novelty in a California Idea Submission Case*, 11 UCLA Ent. L. Rev. 27 (2004).

22 35 U.S.C. § 112(b).
23 *See* John W. Shaw Advertising, Inc. v. Ford Motor Co., 112 F. Supp. 121 (N.D. Ill. 1953) (concreteness required because an abstract idea cannot be enforced as a property interest).
24 68 F. Supp. 13 (S.D.N.Y. 1946).
25 Flemming v. Ronson Corp., 258 A.2d 153 (N.J. Super. Ct. 1969).
26 Dewey v. American Stair Glide Corp., 557 S.W.2d 643 (Mo. Ct. App. 1977).
27 Tate v. Scanlan Int'l, Inc., 403 N.W.2d 666 (Minn. Ct. App. 1987).
28 210 F.2d 706 (D.C. Cir. 1953).
29 88 Cal. Rptr. 679 (Cal. Ct. App. 1970).
30 541 P.2d 663 (Nev. 1975).
31 *See* Shanco Int'l, Ltd. v. Digital Controls, Inc., 312 S.E.2d 150 (Ga. Ct. App. 1983).
32 85 N.Y.S.2d 51 (N.Y. Mun. Ct. 1941).
33 14 N.E.2d 388 (N.Y. 1938).
34 *See* Galanis v. Procter & Gamble Corp., 153 F. Supp. 34 (S.D.N.Y. 1957).
35 *See* Jones v. Ulrich, 95 N.E.2d 113 (Ill. Ct. App. 1950).
36 319 P.2d 776 (Cal. Ct. App. 1957).

5 Scope of liability for idea theft

Settling on a legal theory of idea protection and available claims is only the initial step in an idea theft case. The plaintiff must make a demand for a remedy and then prove his or her case. It is also advisable that the plaintiff anticipate any potential defenses that the defendant might assert in response. Plaintiffs in idea theft cases usually seek monetary compensation as a remedy for the unauthorized use of their idea. Regardless of whether the action is a contract or property-based claim, if successful, the plaintiff can recover the amount of actual damages as measured by the reasonable or fair market value of the idea or the amount of the defendant's profits.

It is also possible in idea theft cases to obtain injunctive relief prohibiting the defendant from using or disclosing the plaintiff's idea. The plaintiff must offer proof of irreparable harm in order to be granted an injunction.[1] In idea theft property-based misappropriation claims, the plaintiff may seek punitive damages; however, courts do not award punitive damages for breach of express or implied contracts. Irrespective of the legal theory that underlies the idea originator's claim for damages or injunctive relief, the defendant is liable only if the idea he or she used was the same one that originated with and was submitted by the plaintiff.

Recipient's use of the idea

A plaintiff in an idea theft case must prove that the recipient actually used the idea without authorization. A plaintiff cannot recover for misappropriation of ideas unless the ideas are actually used by a defendant. In *McGhan v. Ebersol*,[2] the plaintiff claimed to have created and submitted several ideas for segments to be used on a new music video television show, which was eventually known as "Friday Night Videos." After a series of discussions, the producer of the show discontinued his involvement with the plaintiff and he filed suit for misappropriation of his ideas. However, the claims failed because the plaintiff admitted that several ideas were never actually used on the show and he was unable to demonstrate that the remaining ideas were original and not already in use in the industry.[3]

The use of another's idea without permission can be proved by direct evidence, such as an admission by the recipient, or by eyewitness testimony or records documenting the recipient's use of the plaintiff's idea. Alternatively, the recipient's unauthorized use may result from a breach of an express promise to pay for the idea. Where the recipient does not admit to using the plaintiff's idea, or there is no express contract or other direct proof, the plaintiff may prove use by circumstantial evidence that the recipient had access to the idea and that the defendant's idea or product is identical or substantially similar to the plaintiff's idea. If so, this creates an inference that the recipient had a reasonable opportunity to hear or view the idea and then used it by copying or developing it. For an express contract claim, however, the level of similarity permitting an inference of use is tied to the language of the parties' agreement.[4]

Access can be understood as the reasonable possibility that the defendant viewed or heard the plaintiff's idea. For instance, the defendant may have read the plaintiff's proposal or treatment, or may have attended a pitch session where it was presented. However, evidence of access cannot be speculative. Access could not be inferred merely because a copy of the idea was submitted to the defendant, or that it was received at the defendant's place of business, without proof that it was received and of the chain of events or custody that establishes that the defendant had a reasonable opportunity to view or hear the idea. This is illustrated in *Mann v. Columbia Pictures, Inc.*,[5] where the plaintiff wrote an outline describing an idea for a movie and submitted it to the neighbor of a friend, who passed it along to a production manager at a production company that was financially associated with but not part of Columbia Pictures. He passed it on to a story editor at the production company who was not employed by Columbia Pictures. When Columbia released the movie "Shampoo" a few years later, the plaintiff noted similarities between the plot and her outline and filed a breach of implied contract action against Columbia. On appeal, the court noted the speculative and conjectural nature of the argument that her outline had somehow found its way to Columbia's production department and rejected her claim.

Moreover, access alone does not create an inference of actual use unless there is similarity between the idea and the defendant's idea or product. The level of similarity is not identity or near identity between the plaintiff's idea and what the defendant has produced. Rather, the requirement is met by finding that there are enough similarities so that a reasonable person is able to conclude that the defendant used the idea. Of course, the greater the similarity, the more likely a reasonable person would conclude that the defendant used the plaintiff's idea. A high level of similarity as to the details or specifics makes the conclusion more probable that the defendant used the plaintiff's idea. This standard of proof is essentially the same used to prove the element of copying in a copyright infringement action.[6] Copying is proved when the plaintiff demonstrates that the defendant had access to the copyrighted work and that there are enough probative resemblances between them to be similar.[7]

The case of *Benay v. Warner Bros. Entertainment, Inc.*[8] provides a useful illustration. The plaintiffs were authors of a screenplay entitled "The Last Samurai" and their agent "pitched" the screenplay and provided a copy to the defendant, a production company. The defendant decided to "pass" on the submission on the basis that it already had a similar project in development. Two years later, the defendant released a film entitled "The Last Samurai," which bore the same title as well as a number of other similarities to the plaintiffs' screenplay. In both works, for instance, the protagonist was an embittered American war veteran who travels to Japan where he meets the Emperor, trains the Imperial Army in modern warfare, fights against the samurai, and in the end is spiritually restored. The plaintiffs filed suit for copyright infringement and idea theft based on breach of implied contract. The court found no copyright infringement because the two works were not substantially similar as to their expressive elements. However, the court ruled that the works were similar enough to find the defendants in breach of an implied contract for using the plaintiffs' plot idea, theme, historical facts, and related stock elements without payment.

By contrast, in *Reginald v. New Line Cinema Corp.*,[9] the plaintiff authored a book entitled "The Party Crasher's Handbook" detailing his personal experiences crashing celebrity parties and events around Los Angeles, and describing a wedding he had crashed. In 1999, he decided to submit the book and a synopsis to movie producers, and eventually had a conversation with a producer at New Line Cinema in which he told him about his idea. New Line responded a short time later that it was not interested in the concept. However, in 2004, the plaintiff discovered that New Line was planning to release a movie entitled "Wedding Crashers," a comedy about two bachelors who crash weddings and become romantically involved with women they meet at a wedding. He filed an action for breach of implied contract and breach of confidence against New Line. However, the court concluded that an overall comparison of the plaintiff's idea and the movie revealed that there was no substantial similarity between them. The idea in the plaintiff's book was that crashing a wedding was one of several different types of events to crash, but the movie used wedding crashing merely to set the stage for the primary story of the friendship between the two main characters and the romantic relationships they develop. The only similarities were that both included wedding crashing and the incidents and settings common to wedding events.

The "Blurt-Out" defense

Neither the submission of an unsolicited idea itself, nor the fact that the idea may be valuable, will lead to liability on the basis of breach of contract. When an idea originator discloses an unsolicited idea before the recipient knows and agrees that compensation was a condition for use of the idea, the courts will not recognize an implied contract. In *Desny v. Wilder*[10] the California Supreme Court delineated what has come to be known as the "blurt-out" defense: "Unless the offeree has opportunity to reject he cannot be said to accept."[11] Therefore, if the idea originator simply "blurts out" the idea to the recipient unsolicited, no contract can be implied.[12]

The blurt-out defense to implied contract and breach of confidence claims is illustrated in *Keane v. Fox Television Stations, Inc.*[13] In this case, the plaintiff had developed an idea for a televised talent show to be entitled "American Idol" and composed a treatment and related information describing the idea. He then mass-mailed these materials to prospective financial investors and production companies, and posted it on the Internet to generate interest. One of the recipients of the materials subsequently developed and sold the concept for the "American Idol" talent show to Fox Television. When the plaintiff brought suit for breach of implied contract, the court dismissed the claim, pointing out that if an idea was disclosed unsolicited and without notice to the recipient, then no implied contract or obligation of confidentiality will be found. The plaintiff had "blurted out" his idea while promoting it and had not communicated that he expected compensation in return for disclosing the idea.

Once bargaining between the parties begins, with the recipient aware that the idea originator expects to be paid in return for disclosure, the blurt-out defense is not available. As an example, consider the case of *West v. eBay, Inc.*,[14] which involved a plaintiff who created a business plan for his auction marketplace valet service. He emailed documents to the defendant describing the idea, and the defendant later launched a similar service. When sued, among other claims, for breach of express contract, the defendant argued that the plaintiff had blurted out his idea by emailing it and thereby negating its novelty. The court disagreed, finding that the plaintiff's complaint alleged that he and the defendant's agents had conversations making use of the business plan conditional on the plaintiff being compensated as a consultant prior to the email. This foreclosed dismissal of claim on the basis of the blurt-out defense.[15]

The result in West is consistent with that in *Smith v. Snap-On Tools Corp.*,[16] in which the plaintiff disclosed his idea for a new ratchet on his own initiative without any prompting from the defendant and without making it clear that the disclosure was intended as part of a negotiation aimed at creating a licensing agreement or entering into a similar business transaction. Nor did the plaintiff ever request confidentiality in any of his dealings with the defendant. As a consequence, the court rejected the plaintiff's claim for compensation, explaining that reliance on confidentiality must exist at the time the disclosure is made and an attempt to establish a confidential relationship after an initial disclosure is too late.

The independent development defense

Even if the plaintiff has presented evidence of access and similarity, the independent development defense allows a defendant to defeat a claim for compensation by an idea provider. This is true regardless of whether the disputed idea is identical to the submitted idea. An idea recipient may avoid liability by proving that the same idea had been acquired from another source or that the recipient developed the same idea independently. To do so, the defendant must demonstrate that he or she had no knowledge of or access to the plaintiff's idea and document the independent creation or discovery of the same idea. Proof of independent development will rebut an inference that the defendant has unlawfully used the plaintiff's idea.

The independent development defense can be understood as the obverse of the novelty requirement, since an idea already known or possessed by the defendant is by definition not novel, either generally or to the recipient. It also demonstrates that the idea in dispute is not original in the sense that it originated through the defendant's efforts independent of what the plaintiff may have submitted. Moreover, the defense is consistent with similar defenses in trade secret and copyright law. A person who independently invents or discovers new information identical to another's trade secret, without relying on improper means to do so, is not liable for trade secret misappropriation.[17] A defendant in a copyright infringement case can rebut an inference of copying by proving that he or she independently created an identical or substantially similar work.[18]

The defense was first applied in *Teich v. General Mills*,[19] which involved a claim for breach of implied contract based on an allegation by the plaintiff that the defendant used his idea for a cereal box prize. The plaintiff had presented his idea for a toy camera for making sun pictures on condition of payment if the defendant used his idea. When the plaintiff discovered several months later a package of the defendant's cereal containing the same toy as a prize, he sued. The defendant introduced uncontradicted evidence that it had optioned the same idea from an advertising agency before the plaintiff submitted his idea. The court stated that proof of independent development of the same idea negates an inference that the defendant copied the plaintiff's idea.

The *Downey v. General Foods Corp.*[20] case involves the application of the independent development defense in an idea misappropriation case and illustrates the importance of the defendant's internal procedures in avoiding liability. The plaintiff submitted an idea to General Foods suggesting that General Foods' "Jell-O" product be renamed "Wiggley" or "Mr. Wiggle" in marketing the product to children. General Foods replied that it was not interested in his concept. However, when General Foods later promoted its product for sale using the name "Mr. Wiggle," Downey sued to recover damages for misappropriation of his idea. General Foods appealed after the district court denied its motion for summary judgment. On appeal, the court reversed based on evidence that General Mills had generated the same idea and used it in advertising years before the plaintiff had submitted it. Consequently, the idea was neither novel nor original. Both Teich and Downey underscored the importance of documenting independent creation with clear and uncontradicted evidence.[21]

Notes

1 *See* Cargo Protectors, Inc. v. American Lock Co., 92 F. Supp.2d 926 (D. Minn. 2000).

2 608 F. Supp. 277 (S.D.N.Y. 1985).

3 *Accord* Galanis v. Proctor & Gamble Corp., 153 F. Supp. 34 (S.D.N.Y. 1957).
4 *See* Ryder v. Lightstorm Ent't, Inc., 201 Cal. Rptr.3d 110 (Cal. Ct. App. 2016).
5 180 Cal. Rptr. 522 (Cal. Ct. App. 1982).
6 *See* Kurt M. Saunders, Intellectual Property Law: Legal Aspects of Innovation and Competition 377–79 (2016).
7 *Id.*
8 607 F.3d 620 (9th Cir. 2010).
9 2008 WL 588932 (Cal. Ct. App. 2008).
10 299 P.2d 257 (Cal. 1956).
11 *Id.* at 272.
12 *Id.* at 270 ("The idea man who blurts out his idea without having first made his bargain has no one but himself to blame for the loss of his bargaining power.") *See also* Jordan-Benel v. Universal City Studios, Inc., 2015 WL 9694896 (C.D. Cal. 2015).
13 297 F. Supp.2d 921 (S.D. Tex. 2004).
14 2017 WL 5991749 (N.D.N.Y. 2017).
15 *See id.* at *4. *Accord* Onza Partners SL v. Sony Pictures Ent't Inc., 2017 WL 8222204 (C.D. Cal. 2017).
16 833 F.2d 578 (5th Cir. 1987).
17 *See* Saunders, *supra* note 5, at 50.
18 *See id.* at 384.
19 339 P.2d 627 (Cal. Ct. App. 1959).
20 286 N.E.2d 257 (N.Y. Ct. App. 1972).
21 *See* Morawski v. Lightstorm Ent., Inc., 599 Fed. Appx. 779 (C.D. Cal. 2013) (defendant produced earlier writings describing same plot idea); Kienzle v. Capital Cities/ABC Co., Inc., 774 F. Supp. 432 (E.D. Mich. 1991) (defendant proved no contact with plaintiff's idea); Mann v. Columbia Pictures, Inc., 180 Cal. Rptr. 522 (Cal. Ct. App. 1982) (proof that defendant had no access to plaintiff's idea in creating the same story concept); Vantage Point, Inc. v. Parker Bros., Inc., 529 F. Supp. 1204 (E.D.N.Y. 1981) (no proof that defendant had stolen an idea for an oil exploration game).

6 Comparative approaches to idea protection

With nearly 200 countries in the world, each with its own body of law, it would be difficult to comprehensively describe how each of them addresses idea theft, or whether they do so at all. Any study of comparative approaches to idea protection must begin with the understanding that the legal system in one country often varies greatly from those in other countries. Broadly speaking, there are currently three modern legal systems in place among the countries of the world, with a number of countries that have a mixed form of legal system. The civil law system, found in most European and Asian countries and the countries of Latin America, is based on the primacy of statute or code-based law embodying the rules that apply to the rights and duties of private persons and transactions between them.[1] The common law system, originating in England and found in most former English colonies and territories, is based on a body of court decisions that serve as precedents for deciding future cases.[2] Finally, the Islamic legal system or Shari'a is a body of law that finds its source in the Koran and other religious teachings and principles, and is found in most Muslim nations.[3]

Protection of ideas under international intellectual property law

Differences in legal systems, as well as cultural traditions and values, are likely to have implications for how the law of a country protects ideas or responds to a claim of idea misappropriation. However, no survey of the comparative law of ideas can begin without acknowledging that a system of international intellectual property law agreements has greatly harmonized the national intellectual property law regimes of signatory countries.[4] Of particular relevance is the Trade-Related Aspects of Intellectual Property Rights (TRIPS) Agreement among the members of the World Trade Organization (WTO).[5] The TRIPS

Agreement is concerned with the protection of intellectual property rights in international trade and with the diffusion of technological innovation by establishing minimum standards of protection for WTO countries.[6] Members of the WTO, such as the United States, are obligated to align their national laws to these standards. Even so, this does not necessarily ensure protection for undeveloped or unused ideas within traditional forms of intellectual property law in WTO countries.

According to article 9.2 of the TRIPS Agreement, copyright applies to expression and does not extend to an idea.[7] Thus, idea originators in any WTO member country will find no protection under copyright law for valuable ideas unless those ideas have been communicated in an expressive work, such as a screenplay, computer program, or a drawing. Unlike the ineligibility of abstract ideas for patent protection under U.S. patent law, the TRIPS Agreement contains no such express exclusion.[8] Nevertheless, WTO members must require that a patent applicant disclose the invention in a manner sufficiently clear and complete for the invention to be carried out by a person skilled in the art, and may require the applicant to indicate the best mode for carrying out the invention.[9] This suggests that an idea that has not be adequately delineated and disclosed is not a patent-eligible invention.

Lastly, article 39.2 of the TRIPS Agreement protects undisclosed information – trade secrets and business know-how – if the information is secret, has commercial value because it is secret, and has been subject to reasonable steps to keep it secret.[10] The owner of secret information must have legal recourse to prevent it from being disclosed to, or acquired or used by, others without his or her consent in a manner contrary to honest commercial practices. "Manner contrary to honest commercial practices" includes breach of contract, breach of confidence and inducement to breach, as well as the acquisition of undisclosed information by third parties who knew, or were grossly negligent in failing to know, that such practices were involved in the acquisition.[11] The TRIPS Agreement does not guarantee that an idea will be protected as a trade secret. Rather, this will be decided under the national law of the WTO member country. If an idea is a trade secret under national law, and it is disclosed to another person subject to a condition of confidentiality, it will be protected from misappropriation if it is used or disclosed without permission. Regardless of the source of trade secrets law, ideas present an uneven fit given the requirements for protection. Recall that ideas that are only novel to the recipient, rather than generally novel, cannot be trade secrets because they are already known by others. Valuable ideas are usually developed with the intent of disclosing them to a recipient, but this must be done pursuant to a confidentiality or nondisclosure agreement or else their status as trade secrets will be lost.

Protection of ideas under national laws

While the member states of the European Union (EU) are also bound by article 39.2 of the TRIPS Agreement, in 2016 the EU adopted the Directive on the Protection of Undisclosed Know-How and Business Information Against Their Unlawful Acquisition, Use, and Disclosure, otherwise known as the EU Trade Secrets Directive. According to the Directive, a trade secret is information that "is secret in the sense that it is not … generally known among or readily accessible to persons within the circles that normally deal with the kind of information in question;" has "commercial value because it is secret"; and "has been subject to reasonable steps under the circumstances, by the person in control of the information, to keep it secret."[12] The definition of trade secrets reflects the wording of article 39(2) and is similar to the definition of trade secrets under the Uniform Trade Secrets Act (UTSA) in the United States.[13] In addition, the Directive's definition of misappropriation as the "unlawful acquisition, use, or disclosure of trade secrets" is consonant with the TRIPS Agreement and the UTSA.[14] As with the TRIPS Agreement, the EU Trade Secrets Directive does not mandate that ideas be treated as trade secrets, so the protection of ideas, either under the Directive or within the rubric of other legal theories, remains a matter of national law.

The United Kingdom presents an illustrative case in point. Although it is possible that some ideas will meet the prerequisites for treatment as trade secrets in the U.K., it is more likely that idea disclosures will be more easily protected under a breach of confidence theory. Before it departed the European Union, the U.K. implemented the EU Trade Secrets Directive even though British common law has long protected confidential information.[15] When information is disclosed in confidence, either explicitly or implicitly, the recipient is subject to an obligation of confidentiality and there is a legal remedy if the recipient makes unauthorized use or disclosure of the information.[16] Confidential information is broader than trade secrets[17] and can encompass any information that is not already common knowledge or in the public domain like novel ideas.[18] The elements of proving an action for breach of confidence are that (1) the information must be confidential, (2) the disclosure of the information must have been in circumstances which give rise to an obligation of confidence, and (3) there must be an actual or anticipated unauthorized use or disclosure of the information.[19] In other words, the recipient of confidential information is not allowed to use it as a springboard for his or her own gain or for activities detrimental to the idea submitter.[20]

Indeed, breach of confidence has been recognized as the basis of a claim for idea misappropriation cases in the UK. In *Fraser v. Thames Television Ltd.*,[21] the plaintiffs formulated an idea for a television series based on the story of three female rock singers who formed a band. They discussed the idea with Thames Television and offered Thames the right of first refusal on the idea, conditional on three of the plaintiffs who were actresses being cast as the three rock singers. When Thames made the program without casting the actresses, the plaintiffs brought a claim for breach of confidence. Thames argued that the idea disclosed was not protected unless it was a developed idea that had been recorded in some permanent form. The court disagreed, holding that the idea only need be sufficiently developed to be understood as a concept, and that it must be novel and not a matter of public knowledge.[22]

Likewise, in *Wade v. British Sky Broadcasting, Ltd.*,[23] the plaintiffs pitched an idea to Sky television for a music talent show called "The Real Deal" premised on the contestants who, as singer-songwriters, would perform their own original songs rather than cover versions to earn prizes. The idea was pitched using a deck of digital slides. Although Sky expressed some initial interest, it declined the idea. Later, Sky began producing its own show called "Must Be the Music" with a similar, though not identical, format. The plaintiffs filed suit for breach of confidence, arguing that "Must Be the Music" had been derived from their idea. Sky argued that the information did not qualify as confidential information and that even if it was confidential, it had independently developed its own show. The court agreed that "The Real Deal" had been conveyed to Sky in circumstances where an obligation of confidentiality was implied, and the idea contained in the slides as a whole was confidential information, but also found that Sky presented convincing evidence that its show had been created independently and was therefore not liable for breach of confidence.

As in the United States, an idea may be disclosed subject to an express or implied contract requiring confidentiality. In such cases, unauthorized use or disclosure can form the basis for a breach of contract action. Furthermore, the *Fraser* and *Wade* cases demonstrate the similarities of U.K. and U.S. law as to a claim for breach of confidence. As in the United States, ideas are protectable in the United Kingdom if they are sufficiently novel and concrete. Moreover, if the idea is received under conditions of confidentiality, it cannot be used or disclosed without permission. Nevertheless, the defendant can avoid liability if there is evidence that he or she independently created or developed the same or similar idea.[24]

The law of breach of confidence as applied to ideas has broadly followed suit in other British Commonwealth nations. Liability for breach of confidence sometimes accompanies claims for copyright infringement. In the Canadian case of *Hutton v. Canadian Broadcasting Corporation*,[25] for example, the plaintiff conceived of a television program called "Star Tracks." He persuaded the CBC network to co-produce with him a program called "Star Charts" based upon his idea and Hutton retained copyright in the show as a dramatic work. When the CBC cancelled the show and subsequently produced and aired a similar show entitled "Good Rockin' Tonite," Hutton brought a copyright infringement action against the CBC, along with a claim for breach of confidence, but was unsuccessful due to lack of substantial similarities between the two shows.

By contrast, in the New Zealand case of *Wilson v. Broadcasting Corporation of New Zealand*,[26] the plaintiff conceived of a concept for an animated television series entitled "The Kiwi Kids" in which the main characters were a physically disabled boy and girl who engaged in heroic adventures. The plaintiff forwarded a nine-page treatment to the defendant television network. When the defendant premiered an animated series entitled "The Kids from OWL" involving a physically disabled boy and girl who engaged in crime-hting adventures, the plaintiff sued and the case made its way to the New Zealand High Court. The Court held that the show format as expressed in the treatment was protected by copyright as a dramatic work and had been infringed, but also held that the defendant was liable for breach of confidence as to the concept itself.

Finally, in contrast to the common law approach to idea protection taken by common law systems, South Korea has opted for statutory redress for the misappropriation of valuable ideas. The Korean Unfair Competition Prevention and Trade Secret Protection Act[27] prohibits idea theft as a form of unfair competition. Included within the definition of "unfair competition" is the following:

> An act of unfairly using information which includes another person's technical or business ideas with economic value in the process of negotiating or conducting transactions such as a business proposal, auction, and public offering for his or her business interests or the business interests of a third party in violation of the purpose of the provision or an act of providing such information

> to another person so that he or she can take advantage of it: Provided, That this shall not apply if the person provided with such ideas is already knowledgeable about them or such ideas are well known in the relevant industry … .[28]

There are exceptions for ideas that are already known by the recipient at the time they were submitted, and for ideas well known in the same field or industry. Before the enactment of this provision of the statute, ideas and concepts, standing alone, were protected only by way of contracts. The statute allows for injunctive relief and compensatory damages against a defendant who has taken advantage of an idea created and developed by another.[29]

Notes

1 *See* H. Patrick Glenn, Legal Traditions of the World 116–156 (2000).
2 *See id.* at 205–250.
3 *See id.* at 157–204.
4 For a comprehensive review of these international agreements, see generally Susy Frankel & Daniel J. Gervais, Advanced Introduction to International Intellectual Property (2016).
5 WTO Agreement on Trade-Related Intellectual Property Rights, Marrakesh Agreement Establishing the World Trade Organization, Annex 1C, Apr. 15, 1994, in World Trade Organization, The Legal Texts: The Results of the Uruguay Round of Multilateral Trade Negotiations (1999), as amended Jan. 23, 2017 (hereinafter TRIPS Agreement).
6 *See* Kurt M. Saunders, Intellectual Property Law: Legal Aspects of Innovation and Competition 762–774 (West Academic 2016).
7 TRIPS Agreement, art. 9.2.
8 Article 27(1) of the TRIPS Agreement provides that patents "shall be available for any inventions, whether products or processes, in all fields of technology." *Id.* art. 27(1). "[P]atents shall be available for any inventions, whether products or processes, in all fields of technology, provided that they are new, involve an inventive step and are capable of industrial application." *Id.* An "inventive step" and "capable of industrial application" are equivalent to the requirements of nonobviousness and utility under U.S. patent law. *See id.* n.5.
9 *Id.* art. 29(1).
10 *Id.* art. 39(2). The information must be secret because it is not known or readily accessible to persons who normally deal with such information. *Id.*
11 *Id.* n.10.
12 Art. 2, Directive 2016/943, of the European Parliament and of the Council of 8 June 2016 on the Protection of Undisclosed Know-How and Business Information (Trade Secrets) Against Their Unlawful Acquisition, Use and Disclosure 2016 O.J. (L 157) 18 (hereinafter EU Directive).
13 Unif. Trade Secrets Act § 1(4) (amended 1985), 14 U.L.A. 538 (2005).
14 EU Directive, art. 4.

15 Implementation occurred in the form of the Trade Secrets Regulations, SI 2018/597.

16 The duty of confidentiality is determined from the standpoint of whether an objective, reasonable person knows or should know that the information is confidential. *See* Vestergaard Frandsen A/S v. Bestnet Europe, Ltd. [2013] U.K.S.C. 31.

17 *See, e.g.*, JN Dairies, Ltd. v. Johal Dairies, Ltd. [2009] E.W.H.C. 1331 (Ch); Stephens v. Avery [1988] 1 Ch. 449.

18 *See* Mustad, O. & Sons v. Dosen [1963] R.P.C. 41.

19 *See* Saltman Eng'g Co., Ltd. v. Campbell Eng'g Co., Ltd. [1948] 65 RPC 203; Coco v. A.N. Clark [Engineers] Ltd. [1969] R.P.C. 41; BBC v. Harper Collins Publishers, Ltd. [2010] EWHC 2424 (Ch), [2011] EMLR 103. This suggests that an idea that has been "blurted out" has not be disclosed in confidence.

20 Terrapin, Ltd. v. Builders' Supply Co., 1960 R.P.D. & T.M. 128 (Eng. C.A.). In addition, novelty of the information is required in a breach of confidence claim. *Id.*

21 [1984] 1 Q.B. 44.

22 *Id.*

23 [2014] E.W.H.C. 634.

24 For a detailed discussion of U.S. and U.K. law on idea protection, see Ronald Caswell, *A Comparison and Critique of Idea Protection in California, New York, and Great Britain,* 14 Loy. L.A. Int'l & Comp. L.J. 717 (1992).

25 [1992] 120 A.R. 291.

26 [1990] 2 N.Z.L.R. 565.

27 Pujong Kyongjaeng Pangjipop (Unfair Competition Prevention Act), Law No. 3897 of 1986, arts. 10–14, amended by Unfair Competition Prevention Act, Law No. 4478 of 1991.

28 *Id.* art. 2(1)(j)(2). Article 2 applies to novel ideas, which amount to an "outcome achieved through substantial investment or efforts." *See id.*

29 *Id.* art. 4–5. In addition, the Commissioner of the Korean Intellectual Property Office (KIPO) may conduct an investigation or recommend corrective action. *See id.* art. 7–8. However, the law specifically excludes the wrongful use of ideas from criminal punishment. *See id.* art. 18(3)(1).

7 Practical aspects of idea submissions

Given the challenges involved in protecting ideas and the potential liability stemming from their unauthorized use, the circumstances of an idea submission involve risk for both the idea provider and the recipient. The idea provider will be reluctant to disclose the idea without a promise of compensation from the recipient if he or she uses the idea. The recipient of the idea, on the other hand, will be hesitant to make such a promise without an assurance that the idea is novel or useful. There is also the reality that more than one individual may independently conceive of the same idea at around the same time. This presents the risk of liability to anyone who may have submitted a similar idea. Thus, the dilemma faced by each of the parties is how best to protect their respective interests. However, the law of contracts offers a means for the parties to do this and mitigate the risks involved in an idea submission.

Idea providers: The nondisclosure agreement

Idea originators are often required to disclose their ideas when negotiating with others to secure financing or collaboration in developing the idea. However, the originator of a useful idea should never disclose it without first communicating to the recipient his or her expectation of payment if the disclosed idea is used. Ideally, the parties will agree to enter into an express contract for the disclosure conditioned on compensation for the idea if it is used. Formation of an express contract of this type is more likely to occur when the idea has been solicited, but less likely when the idea is unsolicited. Courts have held that the consideration to support such agreements is that the recipient receives something of value as measured by whether it is at least novel to the recipient.[1] In either case, the recipient's knowledge and understanding that the idea provider expects to be paid for the idea is critical to establishing any claim based on contract law.[2] Even when the idea is unsolicited, an implied contract may result based on the circumstances of the submission. Alternatively, the recipient may accept disclosure pursuant to the terms of an idea or invention submission agreement.

When an idea originator seeks to submit an idea unsolicited, the best approach to protecting the idea is to request that the recipient sign a nondisclosure agreement, also known as a confidentiality agreement, which describes the nature of the idea, states that it is being disclosed in confidence, and the purpose of the disclosure. The agreement should also precisely state what information is covered by the agreement and condition its disclosure on payment if the recipient decides to use the idea. The practical effect of such an agreement is to bind the recipient from disclosing or using the idea without compensating the idea provider. The recipient's understanding that the disclosure is confidential is essential to maintaining an action for breach of confidence. If the idea provider wishes to rely on trade secret protection, a nondisclosure agreement will serve as evidence of a reasonable measure taken to maintain the secrecy of the idea. Although nondisclosure agreements are regularly used in most manufacturing and technology industries, they are not widely accepted in the entertainment industry. Furthermore, depending on the bargaining position of the parties, the recipient may be unwilling to enter into such an agreement.

What if the intended recipient refuses to enter into a nondisclosure agreement? In such circumstances, the idea provider might consider several other strategies for disclosing the idea. For example, the idea could be disclosed in several stages, where a few details of the idea are revealed upfront for free in order to induce the recipient to purchase the entire idea. Another approach to disclosing the idea is to make a nonexclusive disclosure, where the recipient is given a limited period of time in which to purchase the idea or the idea will be submitted to a competitor. In either case, the recipient should be required to acknowledge that the provider expects to be compensated if the idea is used.

Finally, the idea provider should always consider whether an idea in the form of an invention may qualify for patent protection and, if so, file an application prior to disclosing it to the recipient.[3] The term of the patent, if granted, will begin as of the date of the application.[4] At the very least, the idea provider should consider applying for copyright registration for any tangible expression of the idea, as might be the case with a screenplay, advertising jingle, graphic design, or book manuscript. Although registration will not protect the underlying idea or concept itself, it will allow the idea provider to pursue an action for infringement if the recipient uses any of the copyrightable expression without permission.

Idea recipients: The idea submission agreement

Many manufacturers and media companies routinely receive numerous ideas for new products or improvements, slogans, and marketing campaigns – most unsolicited. For idea recipients, the main concern is the risk that reviewing or even acknowledging acceptance of unsolicited ideas might lead to expensive and prolonged litigation involving spurious claims for copyright or patent infringement, breach of contract, or idea theft. In order to avoid or mitigate potential liability, businesses should institute internal procedures for handling the receipt and possible use of unsolicited ideas. In fact, many businesses simply refuse to accept or consider any unsolicited idea submissions and have instituted internal procedures to implement this policy. For instance, in the entertainment industry, it is current practice to return unread all unsolicited submissions and for screenwriters to have representation by an agent before a producer will accept a submission or agree to hear an idea pitched.

For businesses that are willing to consider unsolicited ideas, a useful procedure for handling such submissions is to segregate them from the marketing or research and development divisions within the company so as to allow the recipient to prove the defense of independent development if sued. Another approach is to route all unsolicited submissions to a designated agent, who either returns the submissions unread or screens them as to their potential value to the recipient and passes the potentially useful ideas on for further review. A similar approach involves segregating unsolicited submissions and evaluating them only if the idea provider first agrees to waive or release the recipient from liability. The recipient directs its agent to return unsolicited submissions with a standard waiver or idea submission agreement that disclaims or limits the recipient's liability for using or disclosing the idea and disclaims any confidential relationship between them.

In *Kearns v. Ford Motor Co.*,[5] for example, the plaintiff submitted his design for an electronic intermittent windshield wiper system to Ford Motor Co. after signing an agreement entitled "Confidential Disclosure Waiver." Because the agreement expressly provided that "Ford Motor Company cannot receive suggestions in confidence," the court concluded that the plaintiff's signing of this waiver prevented the formation of any confidential relationship between the parties. Such agreements may also specify that the idea provider will rely on patent or copyright protection exclusively as it may apply to the disclosure or expression of the idea.[6]

Idea submission agreements are express contracts between idea submitters and recipients. They are commonly used in the entertainment industry for instance, and as previously noted, many movie and television studios refuse to accept unsolicited material unless the writer is represented by an agent or the material is submitted through an agent and the writer signs a waiver. In addition, idea submission agreements typically provide that the recipient is not obligated to evaluate the idea but may choose to do so for the purpose of considering whether to purchase it while promising not to disclose it to others. The parties mutually agree under which circumstances payment will be required if the recipient decides to use the idea, or that they will negotiate further as to compensation. Many product manufacturers now include online idea submission forms containing detailed terms on their websites.[7]

Courts usually look to whether the language of submission agreements is specific and unambiguous regarding the idea submitted and the idea provider's waiver of legal rights. For example, if the agreement defines the submission as a screenplay, then the recipient's use of the underlying concept would not require payment of compensation.[8] In *Burten v. Milton Bradley Co.*,[9] which involved an idea for an electronic board game, the court narrowly interpreted a waiver to allow for a breach of confidence claim because the waiver did not explicitly disclaim a confidential relationship between the parties. Instead, the court found that a jury could reasonably imply a promise of confidentiality by the defendant as to the handling and use of an idea for a game while it was in its possession.

By contrast, in *Segan Ltd. v. Hasbro, Inc.*,[10] which involved an unsolicited submission of toy design concepts, the court found that the following language unambiguously precluded the plaintiff's misappropriation and breach of confidence claims: "No confidential relationship is to be established by such Submission or implied from consideration of the submitted material, and the material is not submitted 'in confidence.'" The contract involved in *Segan* also included a provision stating that the idea submitter's rights were limited to its remedies under patent and copyright law and that "[n]o obligation of any kind is assumed by, nor may be implied against Hasbro and/or its subsidiaries unless or until a formal written contract between the parties is signed, and then the obligations will be only as set forth by the terms of such contract."

An important caveat to the enforceability of submission agreements is that overly broad general waivers of contractual or intellectual property rights are likely to be void and unenforceable. In *FASA Corp. v. Playmates Toys, Inc.*,[11] the plaintiff, a toy designer, was invited by Playmate Toys to pitch an idea for an interactive game after signing a nondisclosure agreement form in which he waived "any and all claims of any kind whatsoever, past, present, or future, known or unknown against Playmate Toys, Inc. in any way relating to or connected to the 'idea.'" In subsequent litigation between the parties, the court refused to enforce the waiver of unknown future claims as against public policy, explaining that "[s]uch a waiver would permit a party to violate another's intellectual property rights with impunity in contravention of the clear and longstanding public policies underlying the trademark, copyright, and patent laws."[12]

Likewise, in *Davis v. General Foods Corp.*,[13] which involved an idea and recipe for making and selling fruit flavors to be used in the production of ice cream, the waiver read: "We shall be glad to examine your idea for a new food product, but only with the understanding that the use to be made of it by us, and the compensation, if any, are matters resting solely in our discretion." The court refused to enforce the agreement, declaring it to be illusory and indefinite because General Foods retained an unlimited right to decide whether to perform or not perform a promise of payment if it used the idea.[14] Thus, a waiver should be specific and narrowly drawn to avoid being unreasonable and invalid as a matter of law.

Appendix A.1

Nondisclosure Agreement

This Agreement is entered into on ____________, 20___, between ________________________ (the "Provider"), and ________________________ (the "Recipient"). The parties understand that the Provider has developed certain valuable information, concepts, ideas, or designs, which the Provider considers to be confidential (referred to as the "Idea"); and the Recipient wishes to review the Idea for possible use in its business; and the Provider wishes to disclose this Idea to the Recipient under the terms and mutual promises set forth in this Agreement.

1. **Disclosure**. Provider shall disclose to the Recipient the Idea, which concerns:

____

____.

2. **Purpose**. Recipient agrees that this disclosure is only for the purpose of the Recipient's evaluation to determine its interest in the commercial exploitation of the Idea.

3. **Limitation on Use**. Recipient agrees not to manufacture, market, sell, disclose, or otherwise use or appropriate the disclosed Idea in any way whatsoever, including but not limited to adaptation, imitation, redesign, or modification. Nothing contained in this Agreement gives Recipient any rights whatsoever in and to the Idea.
4. **Confidentiality**. The Recipient agrees not to directly or indirectly disclose, distribute, or use the Idea or related information, documents, or materials received from the Provider. The Recipient understands and agrees that the unauthorized disclosure of the Idea by the Recipient to others would irreparably damage the Provider. As consideration and in return for the disclosure of this Idea, the Recipient agrees to keep secret and hold in confidence the Idea by not disclosing it to any person or entity.
5. **Recipient's Rights on Delivery and Acceptance**. The Provider agrees that the submission and disclosure of Idea to the Recipient is for the evaluation as identified in the Purpose. The Recipient, in its sole discretion, has the unqualified right whether or not to choose to evaluate the Idea, and is under no obligation to do so. If the Recipient chooses to evaluate the Idea, then Recipient shall advise Provider within ____ days after receipt.
6. **Good Faith Negotiations**. If, on the basis of the evaluation of the Idea, Recipient wishes to pursue the exploitation thereof, Recipient agrees to enter into good faith negotiations to arrive at a mutually satisfactory agreement for these purposes. Until and unless such an agreement is entered into, this nondisclosure Agreement shall remain in force.
7. **Entire Agreement:** This is the entire agreement between us. It replaces and supersedes any prior or oral agreements between the parties.
8. **Interpretation and Dispute Resolution:** This Agreement shall be construed and governed by the laws of the State of ____. Any questions or disputes shall be exclusively resolved by either federal or state courts in the State of ___.
9. **Enforceability**. This Agreement is binding on and inures to the benefit of the parties and their respective legal representatives, successors, and assigns. If any provisions of this Agreement is held to be invalid or unenforceable, the remaining provisions remain in effect.

The parties have signed this Agreement on the date stated above.

Provider____________________ Recipient: __________
Submission Received By:

____

Title: ______________

Appendix A.2

Idea Submission Agreement

______________ and our subsidiaries and affiliates (collectively, "we" or "us") understand that you have an idea, proposal concept, project or transaction ("idea") that you think will be of interest to us and that you wish to voluntarily share with us. We are under no obligation to review your idea, but we may choose to do so for the purpose of considering whether to purchase it. You should realize that an idea that is new to you may be known to us, or may be in the public domain, or already in a planning or development stage by us.

1. **No Obligations:** We are not under any obligation to you as to your idea except as may be set forth in a subsequent written agreement between us. Neither of us is under any obligation to execute such an agreement. Except as may then be specifically provided in such a written agreement, we are as free to use any ideas we had already acquired or were developing that are the same as or similar to those submitted by you. No confidential relationship is created or is to be implied from our consideration of the submitted idea, and the idea is not to be considered as submitted "in confidence."
2. **Limited Rights To Your Idea:** To the extent that your idea constitutes intellectual property, you agree that in protecting your idea you shall rely solely on your rights under the patent, trademark, and copyright laws, and that consideration by us of your submission in no way impairs our right to contest the validity of your patent, trademark, or copyright.
3. **No Compensation:** No agreement for compensation shall be implied by our consideration or review of your idea. In addition, you are not entitled to any finders, brokerage, or similar fees from us as to your idea, regardless of any agreement you many have with any third party.
4. **Entire Agreement:** This is the entire agreement between us. It replaces and supersedes any prior or oral agreements between us.
5. **Interpretation and Dispute Resolution:** This Idea Submission Agreement shall be construed and governed by the laws of the State of ____. Any questions or disputes shall be exclusively resolved by either federal or state courts in the State of ___ and

you agree to submit to the jurisdiction of such courts. If any provisions of this Idea Submission Agreement is held to be invalid or unenforceable, the remaining provisions shall remain in effect.

Your Acceptance of the Idea Submission Agreement

I acknowledge that no promises or representations, either oral or written, have been made to me by ________________ concerning my idea. Further, I agree that no change may be made in the Idea Submission Agreement unless it is in writing and signed by both me and ________________. I have read and understand this Idea Submission Agreement and I agree to accept all of the conditions contained in the Idea Submission Agreement.

Your signature: ________________________

Notes

1 *See, e.g.*, Nadel v. Play-By-Play Toys, 208 F.3d 368 (2d Cir. 2000); Apfel v. Prudential-Bache Securities, Inc., 600 N.Y.S.2d 433 (N.Y. Ct. App. 1993).
2 *See* Flemming v. Ronson Corp., 258 A.2d 153, 156–157 (N.J. Super. Ct. 1969).
3 *E.g.*, Liqwd, Inc. v. L'Oreal USA, Inc., 2019 WL 5587047 (Fed. Cir. 2019) (involving a patent application for a method for coloring hair disclosed pursuant to a nondisclosure agreement); Stratienko v. Cordis Corp., 429 F.3d 592 (6th Cir. 2005) (involving a patent application for a catheter design disclosed pursuant to a nondisclosure agreement).
4 35 U.S.C. § 154.
5 203 U.S.P.Q. 884 (E.D. Mich. 1978).
6 *Accord* Hassell v. Chrysler Corp., 982 F. Supp. 515 (S.D. Ohio 1997) (enforcing a waiver of all claims except those based on patent, copyright, or trademark law); Wanberg v. Ocean Spray Cranberries, Inc., 194 U.S.P.Q. 350 (N.D. Ill. 1977) (enforcing waiver of claims based on confidential relationship but not those based on patent or copyright law); Crown Indus v. Kawneer, 335 F. Supp. 749 (N.D. Ill. 1971) (waiver stating that "no confidential relationship is to be created by such submission" enforceable).
7 An idea submission form on a website can be construed as an offer to enter into a unilateral contract. *See* Quaiz v. Rockler Cos., Inc., 2019 WL 2061952 (D. Ore. 2019).
8 The scenario is based on the facts of *Ware v. Columbia Broadcasting Sys.*, 61 Cal. Rptr. 590 (Cal. Ct. App. 1967).
9 763 F.2d 461 (1st Cir. 1985).
10 924 F. Supp. 512 (S.D.N.Y. 1996).
11 892 F. Supp. 1061 (N.D. Ill. 1995).
12 *Id.* at 1068. The court added that "such waivers would stifle creativity and inventiveness and inhibit inventors from presenting their creations to others." *Id.*
13 21 F. Supp. 445 (S.D.N.Y. 1937).
14 *See id.* at 446–447.

Selected bibliography on the law of ideas

For further reference and investigation, this chapter provides a listing of recommended and pertinent books, book chapters, and journal articles on the law of idea protection.

Books

Bryant, Joy L., *Protecting Your Ideas: The Inventor's Guide to Patents* (Academic Press, 1999).

David, L., *Hudson, Protecting Ideas* (Chelsea House Publishing, 2006).

Husch, T., *That's a Great Idea!: The New Product Handbook: How to Get Evaluate, Protect, Develop and Sell New Product Ideas* (Gravity Publishing, 1986).

Frederick, W.M., *From Edison to iPod: Protect Your Ideas and Make Money* (DK, 2007).

Roger, E.S. & Thomas, J.R., *Intellectual Property: The Law of Copyrights, Patents, and Trademarks* (2003).

Book Chapters

Chisum, D. et al., *Understanding Intellectual Property Law, § 6H*, 3rd ed. (LexisNexis, 2015).

Entertainment and Intellectual Property Law, §§ 5:14-:31 (Thomson Reuters, 2019–2020).

Moore, S.M., *The Biz: The Basic Business, Legal and Financial Aspects of the Film Industry*, chapter 16 (Silman-James Press, 2011).

Myers, G., *Principles of Intellectual Property Law*, chapter 19 (West Academic Publishing 2017).

Nimmer, M.B., *Nimmer on Copyright: A Treatise on the Law of Literary, Musical and Artistic Property, and the Protection of Ideas*, volume 5, chapter 19D (Matthew Bender, 1963; David Nimmer, revision author 1985–present).

Patry, W.F., *Patry on Copyright*, chapter 18, § 18:28 (Thomson Reuters, 2007–2019).

Saunders, K.M., *Intellectual Property Law: Legal Aspects of Innovation and Competition*, chapter 8 (West Academic, 2016).

Shanker, J., Guinn, D.E., & Orenstein, H., *Entertainment Law and Business: A Guide to the Law and Business Practices of the Entertainment Industry*, chapter 2 (Juris Publishing, 2008).

Articles

Allison, S.B., What's the Use? A Primer on the Defense of Independent Creation to Combat Allegations of Idea Theft, *Ariz. St. Sports Ent. L.J.*, 1, 94 (2011).

Axelrod, E., Ideas, A Dime a Dozen, or Worth Protection?, *U. Denver Sports Ent. L. J.*, 13, 3 (2012).

Basin, K., "I Could Have Been a Fragrance Millionaire": Toward a Federal Idea Protection Act, *J. Copyright Soc'y U.S.A.*, 56, 731 (2009).

Beckerman-Rodau, A., Are Ideas Within the Traditional Definition of Property?: A Jurisprudential Analysis, *Ark. L. Rev.*, 47, *603* (1994).

Carswell, R., A Comparison and Critique of Idea Protection in California, New York, and Great Britain, *Loyola L.A. Intl. Comp. L.J.*, 14, 717 (1992).

David, M.M., What Is Your Pitch?: Idea Protection is Nothing But Curveballs, *Loy. L.A. Ent. L.J.*, 15, 475 (1995).

Denicola, R.C., The New Law of Ideas, *Harv. J. L. Tech.*, 28, 195 (2014).

Fink, D.E. & Diaz, D.M., Hey, That Was My Idea: Understanding Damages in Idea Submission, *Comm. Lawyer*, 28, 4 (Jun. 2012).

Greene, K.J., Idea Theft: Frivolous Copyright-Lite Claims, or Hollywood Business Model?, *Hastings Sci. Tech. L.J.*, 7, 119 (2015).

Katz, L., A Powers-Based Approach to the Protection of Ideas, *Cardozo Arts Ent. L. J.*, 23, 687 (2006).

Knox, W.O., The Role of Novelty in a California Idea Submission Case, *UCLA Ent't. L. Rev.*, 11, 27 (2004).

Lionel, S.S., The Law of Ideas, Revisited, *UCLA Ent. L. Rev.*, 1, 9 (1994).

Mary LaFrance, Something Borrowed, Something New: The Changing Role of Novelty in Idea Protection Law, *Seton Hall L. Rev.*, 34, 485 (2004).

Miller, A.R., Common Law Protection for Products of the Mind: An "Idea" Whose Time Has Come, *Harv. L. Rev.*, 119, 703 (2006).

Pearson, L., Navigating the Bramble Bush in Idea Submission Cases, *John Marshall J. Intell. Prop. L.*, 4, 36 (2004).

Reitenour, S., The Legal Protection of Ideas: Is It Really a Good Idea?. *WM. Mitchell L. Rev.*, 18, 121 (1992).

Sandler, J.R., Idea Theft and Independent Creation: A Recipe for Evading Contractual Obligations, *Loyola L.A. L. Rev.*, 45, 1421 (2012).

Swarth, P., The Law of Ideas: New York and California Are More Than 3,000 Miles Apart, *Hastings Comm. Ent. L.J.*, 13, 115 (1990).

Tarantino, B., "I've Got This Great Idea for a Show ..." – Copyright Protection for Television Show and Motion Picture Concepts and Proposals, *Intell. Prop. J.*, 17, 189 (2004).

Index

Alice Corp. PTY Ltd. v. CLS Bank International 18
Aliotti v. R. Dakin & Co. 11
Altavion, Inc. v. Konica Minolta Systems Laboratory, Inc. 23–24
Aronson v. Quick Point Pencil Co. 27
Arrow's information paradox 2

Baer v. Chase 38
Bailey v. Haberle Congress Brewing Co. 44
Baker v. Selden 20–21
Barlow, John Perry 2
Benay v. Warner Bros. Entertainment, Inc. 49
Blackmon v. Iverson 13
blurt-out defense 50–51
Bonito Boats, Inc. v. Thunder Craft Boats, Inc. 27
breach of contract 6–10
breach of confidence 11–12, 62
Buchwald v. Paramount Pictures Corp. 6–7
Burten v. Milton Bradley Co. 64

California law 12–13, 41
Chandler v. Roach 44
Compco Corp. v. Day-Brite Lighting, Inc. 26
confidentiality agreement 62
confidential relationship 11–12
contract law 5–11
concreteness requirement 41–44
Copyright Act 19, 28–29
copyright law 19–20
copyright pre-emption 28–31

Dastar Corp. v. Twentieth Century Fox Film Corp. 22
Davies v. Krasna 11, 65
Davis in General Foods Corp. 65
Defend Trade Secrets Act 22
Desny v. Wilder 8, 14, 50
Diamond v. Diehr 32n12–33n12
Downey v. General Foods Corp. 52
Duffy v. Charles Schwab & Co., Inc. 21

European Union Trade Secrets Directive 56
express contracts 6–7

Facebook 3
Faris v. Enberg 9–10
FASA Corp. v. Playmates Toys, Inc. 64–65
Fink v. Goodson-Todman Enterprises, Ltd. 43
Forest Park Pictures v. Universal Television Network, Inc. 8–9
Fraser v. Thames Television Ltd. (UK) 57

Goldstein v. California 28
Gottschalk v. Benson 18

Hamilton National Bank v. Belt 42
HDNet, LLC v. North American Boxing Council 32–33
Healey v. R.H. Macy & Co. 44
Hutton v. Canadian Broadcasting Corp. (Canada) 58

idea: definition 1; expression dichotomy 19; submissions 61–68; theft 47–50
implied contracts 7–10
independent development defense 51–52
idea submission agreement 63–65, 67–68

Jefferson, Thomas 1–2
John W. Shaw Advertising, Inc. v. Ford Motor Co. 13
Johnson v. Benjamin Moore & Co. 23

Keane v. Fox Television Stations, Inc. 9, 50
Kewanee Oil Co. v. Bicron Corp. 27
Kearns v. Ford Motor Co. 63
Korean Unfair Competition Prevention and Trade Secret Protection Act 58–59

Landsberg v. Scrabble Crossword Game Players, Inc. 9
Lanham Act 20
Learning Curve Toys, Inc. v. PlayWood Toys, Inc. 23
legal systems 54

Mann v. Columbia Pictures, Inc. 48
McGhan v. Ebersol 47–48
McKay Consulting, Inc. v. Rockingham Memorial Hospital 23
Metrano v. Fox Broadcasting Co., Inc. 29
Misappropriation of property 12–14
Murray v. National Broadcasting Co. 38

Nadel v. Play-By-Play Toys & Novelties, Inc. 39–41
New York law 12–13, 24, 41
nondisclosure agreement 61–62, 65–67
novelty requirement 37–41

O'Brien v. RKO Radio Pictures, Inc. 42

Patent Act 18
patent law 17–19
patent pre-emption 26–28
pre-emption 17, 25–32

quasi-contracts 10–11

Reginald v. New Line Cinema Corp. 49–50
remedies 47

Sears, Roebuck & Co. v. Stiffel Co. 26
Segan Ltd. v. Hasbro, Inc. 64
Smith v. Recrion 43–44
Smith v. Snap-On Tools Corp. 50
Statute of Frauds 7
Stewart v. World Wrestling Federation Entertainment, Inc. 12
Stromback v. New Line Cinema 23

Teich v. General Mills 52
Thompson v. California Brewing Co. 12
trademark law 20–22
Trade-Related Aspects of Intellectual Property Rights (TRIPS) Agreement 17, 18, 20, 54–56
trade secret pre-emption 31–32
trade secrets law 22–25

unauthorized use of ideas, proof 48–50
Uniform Trade Secrets Act 31
unjust enrichment 10–11

Vent v. Mars Snackfood U.S., LLC 38
Victor G. Reiling Associates v. Fisher-Price, Inc. 12

Wade v. British Sky Broadcasting, Ltd. (UK) 57
Werlin v. Reader's Digest Association, Inc. 10
West v. eBay, Inc. 50
Whitfield v. Lear 40
Wilson v. Broadcasting Corporation of New Zealand (New Zealand) 58
World Trade Organization (WTO) 17, 54
Wrench LLC v. Taco Bell Corp. 30

For Product Safety Concerns and Information please contact our EU representative GPSR@taylorandfrancis.com
Taylor & Francis Verlag GmbH, Kaufingerstraße 24, 80331 München, Germany

www.ingramcontent.com/pod-product-compliance
Lightning Source LLC
Chambersburg PA
CBHW061839220326
41599CB00027B/5334

* 9 7 8 0 3 6 7 7 0 8 0 9 2 *